Books by this Author

Fight On!

The Answer Book

An Understandable History of the Bible

A Practical and Theological Study of The Book of Acts

A Practical and Theological Study of The Gospel of John

Living With Pain

Answers To the Ravings of a Mad Plunger

Job

Reading and Understanding the Variations
Between the Critical Apparatuses of
Nestle's 25th and 26th Editions of
the *Novum Testamentum-Graece*

How To Minister To Youth

Selected Sermons (Vol. I - X)

Life After Y2K

How To Get your Book Published

Fight On!

(Christian School materials)

Table of Contents

For His Pleasure

ISBN 1-890120-11-1

Library of Congress No.
2001-126316

For His Pleasure

Dr. Samuel C. Gipp Th. D.

DayStar Publishing
PO Box 464 • Miamitown, Ohio 45041

Introduction

Our churches are wandering from the straight way. In many the music has degenerated, the dress standards are gone and moral problems have become routine. Amidst this we hear that everything is all right because, "We're winning souls."

Something is wrong. For many, soul winning has become the pretext for many questionable actions. We can look like the world, talk like the world and act like the world, but as long as we are winning souls it is okay.

To justify this imbalance some have manufactured a false doctrine. That is the teaching that soul winning is the **main theme** of the Bible. Soul winning is what we're here for. Soul winning is the most important thing a Christian can do. While soul winning is important it **is not** our main reason for being here.

By no means is this book an effort to curtail the soul winning efforts of God's people. It is, though, an attempt to point believers toward higher spiritual ground. An effort to place their eyes on their Creator and not take them off. An effort to make them realize that soul winning is not the sole duty of Christianity but a small part of a much greater plan God has for them.

CHAPTER ONE

Is Soul Winning the Main Theme of the Bible?

The Importance of Soul Winning

Winning souls is of **major** importance. If to no one else, at least to the soul that is spared an eternity suffering in the literal flames of Hell. It is also to be noted that, even though everything that is necessary to instill faith in a non-believer is resident in Scripture, man was still given a divine mandate in Matthew 28:19 to **personally** see to the task. If we don't do it, it will **not** take place as a natural process. Ample Scripture is available to urge us to **go**. (Matthew 28:19) To go **house to house**. (Acts 2:46) And what will happen to the lost if we are slack in our commitment? (Matthew 25:41) These truths have been echoed for years from pulpits across the nation and around the world.

This book **does not** seek to condemn or dissuade the soul winner. It focuses instead on one small statement that was spawned by an over-zealous soul winner somewhere in the distant past that soul winning is not only important but that it is the **main theme** of the Bible. In other words, it was the main reason God had for creating the universe and His single driving force for putting man on the planet. Furthermore, it begs an answer of the question: "If soul winning **isn't** the main theme of the Bible, what is?"

"If soul winning isn't the main theme of the Bible, what is?"

Why is the answer to this question important? Because, if soul winning **is not** the main theme of the Bible then this erroneous teaching has steered Christianity in a well meaning but errant direction and has innocently thwarted the true theme of Scripture, whatever that might be. We **owe it to our God** to investigate this issue and establish **His main theme** as **our main theme**.

In Search of Answers

The teaching that soul winning is the main theme of Scripture is commonly accepted amongst Fundamentalists. In other words, we are here with one basic purpose: to win souls. This teaching greatly influenced the growth (and decline) of the great fundamental revival of the seventies. During the decade between about 1970 and 1980 independent Baptist churches across America grew at a fantastic rate due to the fervent soul winning campaigns they promoted. Churches built new auditoriums that held thousands of people while church attendance records were regularly broken with new high figures. During this decade the bus ministry came into its own as the single greatest vehicle for reaching more "unreached" numbers. Everyone was instilled with the need to soul win. In fact, you couldn't be right with God if you weren't a soul winner. Books on soul winning techniques and enthusiasm were written by anyone who could afford the ink and paper. Things were grand and the Lord was coming "next year" so there was nothing of any greater importance than winning souls.

Today the fervor of the seventies has subsided somewhat. Many of those huge auditoriums now have the last twenty or thirty rows of pews roped off to push the dwindling crowds closer to the pulpit. Some have been remodeled with fewer, wider spaced rows in an effort to hide the smaller numbers, in effect filling the same auditorium with fewer people. Yet the teaching of the importance of soul winning has never abated. Congregations are still instructed to get out and "win the lost at any cost." New "fastest growing churches in ________" are replacing the older ones with their main theme remaining un-apologetically "Soul Winning!"

All of this is commendable indeed. But the question screams to be answered: "Is soul winning the **main** theme of the Bible?" The typical Fundamentalist will answer without thinking. Such an answer doesn't even require any thought. "Yes! Of course! Soul winning is what we're here for!" It will be quickly pointed out by these proponents of "Soul winning, soul winning, soul winning!" that this is what built our churches. It **must** be right!

Why did God create the universe? Why did He make

True as that may be, **it does not answer the question!** The **main** theme of the Bible refers to God's single, driving motivation for our existence. Why did He create the universe? Why did He make man? What does He want from us more than anything else? The flippant answer: "Soul winning, soul winning, soul winning" just doesn't satisfy these questions. Try forcing soul winning into the answer for any one of them and it doesn't fit.

1. Why did He create the universe? Soul winning!

2. Why did He make man? Soul winning!

3. What does He want from us more than anything else? Soul winning!

You can have as much blind soul winning zeal as you want but you **cannot,** within reason, conclude that soul winning satisfies these questions. Make any feeble excuse you can but you are still faced with the sad fact that soul winning **is not** a valid reason for God's act of creation. Are we to believe that as the creative week of Genesis chapter one ticked by God was even at that moment eagerly anticipating Man's fall? ...**just so He could save him?!** Are we further to believe that the fall of Man was not only the express will but the express **plan** of God? Was God hiding behind a tree in Eden watching the discourse between Satan and Eve and rooting for Satan?! Was He eagerly looking forward to the future opportunity of seeing His only begotten Son crucified to redeem a race that He had predestined to fall? Such perverted suppositions cannot be foisted on our minds even under the standard "God's mind is too great for man to understand" scam. It simply **cannot be** that God desired, no **intended** for

His creatures to be lost just so He could rescue them from a fate He had preordained.

As commendable as soul winning is it simply cannot explain what God's intentions were when He decided on speaking this world into existence. And to miss God's **actual** purpose and replace it with a well-meaning **erroneous** one has two disastrous results. Man is sent off expending all of his energy on the **wrong** goal. And he never focuses his efforts on the right one.

Sad Results of the Wrong Goal

Remember. The goal of this book **is not** to hamper or stop the duty of soul winning. Nor does it seek to trivialize its importance. It deals with one question and one question only: "Is soul winning the **main** theme of the Bible?"If it is not, then its emphasis **above** the true theme is in fact **overemphasis**. We have seen that soul winning alone cannot explain God's reasons or desires for creating us and our universe. Since nothing else is elevated as equal or higher than soul winning this single-minded emphasis must actually be overemphasis of a noble but lesser goal than God's **main desire**. This overemphasis has led to several errant and even sinful consequences.

1. "I cry for souls all the time."

Men desire to be like God. Not to **be** God, but to maintain the same desires and goals. That is considered to be godly and Christlike. Therefore, under the "Soul winning is God's main desire." theory, to be totally committed to soul winning is to have the same goal as God. God is portrayed as sitting up in Heaven wringing His hands over a lost sinner who rejects His offer of salvation. He has purchased a divine gift for each lost individual and fears that it won't be accepted by each desired recipient. He is seen to be ever on the verge of tears at the thought of even one lost soul going to Hell. Therefore, in an effort to mimic this "godly" attribute, the soul winner often tells of his tremendous burden for the lost. He is seemingly overwhelmed by his Godlike love for **every lost soul**.

What they actually do is turn God into a sniveling little mass Who is heartbroken by the hardness of a Christ rejecting sinner.

This unnatural (Of course it's unnatural. It's a **super**natural, Godlike burden!) burden leads to a bunch of hand wringing soul winners who all but **beg** a lost sinner not to reject Christ. Here you have an overzealous, unrealistic soul winner sitting in front of a disinterested lost man crying crocodile tears in an effort to get this poor lost fool to see how much both he and God love him. Some soul winners have actually convinced themselves that they love everybody just as much as God does. Their tears are God's own tears. Their heartbreak is a mirror of God's. They are one with God. They and God share the same desires, burdens and goals. (It just doesn't get any better than this!)

But what they actually do is turn God into a sniveling little mass Who is heartbroken by the hardness of a Christ rejecting sinner. What is God's **true** position on the lost? Psalm 2:4 says, *He that sitteth in the heavens shall laugh: the Lord shall have them in derision.* If it's possible for you to conjure up a thought without the use of your television try this: On August 6, 1945 the U.S. Air Force dropped an atomic bomb on the Japanese city of Hiroshima. Three days later, on August 9, they dropped a second device on Nagasaki. Now what do you suppose the American peace negotiators said to the Japanese on August 10th? Do you think they sat down, began to wring their hands and weep as they **begged** the Japanese to surrender? Did they say, "Oh please, please don't reject this offer of peace. Oh I just can't stand the thought of your suffering if you do." **Never!** You can bet that they confidently sat down and basically asked, "Want to see another mushroom?"

The overemphasis on soul winning has caused us to present God as a sniveling, whimpering, quivering mass of Jell-O Who will be absolutely crushed by the rejection of a single, hard-hearted sinner. This simply is not the case. Anyone fool enough to reject God's offer of salvation through the death, burial and resurrection of Jesus Christ is **rightfully** headed for a lake of fire. They deserve it. They have it coming. Quit acting like you're heartbroken when you're not. There are some folks who are going to go to Hell serving their god and they thoroughly deserve it. The evil people in Hollywood, Washington DC and elsewhere **knowingly** serve the devil and fully deserve the damnation they earn from damning young people and innocent lost folks.

2. "Hate the sin. Love the sinner."

This loathsome statement is often recited by brainless individuals who think that it is a description of the kind of love God has for all mankind. Pretending to possess the same "Divine" love makes them feel Godlike.

These mindless folks will quickly step up to the defense of a flaming homosexual with this glib remark. They will deeply resent anyone who seems not to share their "godly" compassion for these perverted individuals. In fact, they will find far more malice in their heart for the "uncompassionate" preacher than for the perpetrator of this vile sin. They will suddenly become vicious and judgmental if the "offending" preacher refuses to repent and join them in their "love" for the sinner. Thus we have many well-meaning but misguided Christians today who are tolerating this and other heinous sins in an effort to present themselves as equal with God in their "hatred for the sin but love for the sinner." You had better read Proverbs 6:16-19. Note the word "hate" is directed to the perpetrators of these acts and not to the acts themselves. Apparently there are times when God "hates the sinner."[1] If you think that God "loves" Howard Stern but "hates" his sin you had better get your poor head out of that hole in the ground. If you think that God "loves" Larry Flynt but "hates" his sin you need to start sniffing glue so that you have a reason for your inability to think straight. (And you had certainly better note that God **hates** people that split churches by sowing discord among brethren.)

---

1 Psalm 7:11 makes God's attitude toward the wicked quite clear while Psalm 37:12, 13 tell of God's plans for the wicked. Psalm 34:16 is certainly not a description of a God in anguish over the lost. Look at it. Doesn't exactly sound like He's wringing His hands over their lost condition. Does it? But then, don't you think that with the death of His Son that **He's done enough!?**

3. "Thank God for sin!"

This is no joke. I actually heard a leading soul winning preacher make this statement. His thrust was, "Thank God for sin! If it hadn't been for sin we'd never be lost. And if we were never lost we could never experience the joy of being saved." (God help us!)

This teaching is exactly the same as that of the Roman Catholic Church. The Catholic church calls Adam's sin; "Blessed Sin" because it opened the door for redemption.

People! Get a grip! Sin is not "blessed.' And it is nothing to "thank" God for. Put down your remote and **think!** We have all been in church services where a preacher got up and told of his jaded past. He was a dope addict or pusher. He was a biker. He was vile in every imaginable way. But he has now been washed in the Blood. He is saved. Thank God that he has been redeemed. But unfortunately this kind of testifying sometimes leads our children, those who were saved at a young age **before** entering such a life to think that they have no testimony. Although this testimony is **good** there is a **better** one.

Many years ago I was having a discussion with a fellow Christian. He was 6" 4" tall and weighed about 225 pounds. Though docile in nature he was fearless in his stand for Christ and had even physically laid hands on some bikers where he worked for making vile comments about his wife. Yet he **still** had the blush of innocence on his face. He was raised on a farm in Pennsylvania in a Christian home. His parents, both saved, took him and his brothers and sisters to

It is better to have never been dirty than to have been dirty and had to get cleaned up.

church every Sunday. He was saved at an early age. He looked at me and **not self-righteously** said, "Preacher, I've never held a cigarette in my hands. I've never tasted booze." **That's the best testimony!!!** It is better to have **never been dirty** than to have been dirty and had to get cleaned up. It would have been **better** if Adam and Eve **had never sinned** than for them to have sinned and needed redemption. No! We have no business "thanking" God for sin! We should thank Him for those who got saved early enough not to have been dirtied and scarred by it.

Yet this abstract approach to the "value" of sin leads to a conclusion that no hyper-soul winner dare acknowledge. Think! (Can you?) If soul winning is the main theme of the Bible then Man needed to be lost so **the devil** did God a great service by causing Man to fall. But wait! It gets worse. God wanted Jesus to die for our sins. Therefore **the real hero** of Scripture is **Judas**. Why if Judas hadn't done us all that great favor of betraying Christ **He might never have died for our sins!** Thank God for sin! Thank God for the devil! Thank God for Judas! (Thank God He doesn't **kill** people for being stupid or the ranks of Christianity would thin drastically overnight!)

I say again. It would have been better for Adam and Eve to have **never** sinned. It was not God's intention for them to fall. It was not His desire that they die. He had a much higher goal for them. One in line with His true main theme of Scripture.

4. Immoral soul winners

Strangely, as much as some preachers display their great "Godlike" burden for the lost they seem to be totally incapable of living morally. The reports of pastors, evangelists and missionaries committing adultery are too numerous to count and too obvious to ignore. But how could someone who was fulfilling the "main theme" of the Bible live so loosely? They live that way for the very reason mentioned. Because they teach that soul winning is the single, most important thing any Christian can do they feel that the "good" they do by soul winning is greater than the "bad" they do by committing adultery! This is no idle statement. Some soul winners, after having been caught in an illicit affair, have made that very declaration! Their "little" immorality does not outweigh the "greater good" they are doing by winning so many people to Christ. Again, this perverted conclusion comes from **overemphasizing** such a noble undertaking as keeping people out of Hell. But it **does not** justify sin!

5. Rubber stamp conversions

More than one person in the wake of a hyper-soul winner is "Saved and going to Hell." If soul winning is the ultimate goal then the more folks you have saved the more you are in the will of God. This leads to such foolishness as claims of winning 200 and 300 or more souls **per week!** It leads to such foolishness as slowly nodding your head as you witness in order to get your listener to accept your witness.

"If they didn't have a chance to say, 'No.' they didn't have a chance to say, 'Yes.'"

One famous soul winner tells his apprentices to "Just bow your head and start praying. This will

embarrass them into bowing their head and praying the sinner's prayer."

I once had a conversation with a very zealous soul winning friend. He said he was instructed "not to give them a chance to say 'No' when winning souls." I told him, "If they didn't have a chance to say, 'No.' they didn't have a chance to say, 'Yes.'" If there is no option for "no" then no **decision** has been made.

Imagine going down to your local car dealer to "window shop." You sit in a beautiful new sedan as the salesman, slowly nodding his head says, "You like this car. Don't you." "Yep! It surely is a nice one." With that you leave the dealership and return home. The next day the salesman pulls the shiny new sedan into your driveway and says, "Here's the new car you bought. You own me $35,000." You protest, "I never said I wanted that car!" To which the sly salesman responds, "But you never said you didn't."

People, such careless treatment of immortal souls has led to millions who are on their way to Hell after repeating a meaningless prayer with a slick soul winning "salesman." They are lost but will hang on to that worthless, deceitful prayer all the way to Hell. In defense of such tactics, one leading soul winner stated, "I like the way I'm doing it better than the way you're **not** doing it!" But wouldn't it be an awful thing to get to Heaven only to find that you put more people into Hell than you did into Heaven...**all with the same prayer!?**

6. Tracts written to please Christians

To the hyper-soul winner **"all that matters is souls!"** Therefore anything that is not geared to winning the lost is worthless and near apostate. Nowhere is this more evident than in our tracts.

It doesn't take a genius to see that **thinking** has become almost non-existent in America today. Most Americans quit thinking the day after they got their

A fourteen year old boy who admits to being an atheist shoots and kills four teens while they're praying and the News Industry tyrants are silent.

television set. Now their brain is operated by a remote. They don't think anymore. They just tune in a news program and are told what their opinion is. Examples of this are everywhere. Howard Stern can puke up his vile imagination for all to hear but the News Industry doesn't condemn him so neither does the American public. But Reggie White states that homosexuality is a sin and the intolerant News Mafia goes ballistic...and so does the public. Even **Christians** are heard to whine that he wasn't being "charitable"! Police beat a vile law breaker into submission who happens to be black and it's a "hate crime" cries the hate-filled News Industry. Yet when a fourteen year old boy who admits to being an atheist shoots and kills four teens **while they're praying** the News Industry tyrants are silent. And thoughtless Americans obediently parrot whatever their News Industry masters place in their heads.

The Bible says *If the foundations be destroyed, what can the righteous do?* (Ps. 11:3) America needs to have its **foundations** repaired. Yet any tract that dealt solely with the Christian heritage of our country, or the need to bring back cleanliness, or ethics would be condemned by Fundamentalism as modernist and apostate if it didn't make soul winning rather than inspiring thought as its primary goal. If it doesn't contain a "1-2-3 repeat after me" prayer it is condemned. Thus, Christians **who don't think** condemn lost folks **who don't think** to a thoughtless existence. So, they just go out and party merrily without a clue to who their greatest enemy is in this country.

7. God can't be trusted

Those who feel compelled to win a person the first time they witness to them cannot bring themselves to trust **God** to work on that person. They cry, "But what if he dies before I get to witness to him again?" The answer is twofold. "He will go to Hell where he deserves to go." and "Do you think he can die without God knowing about it?" Can't God be trusted, I mean **trusted,** to continue a witness after we leave? Can't He be trusted to keep our lost friend alive while He deals with him. You don't really believe that God is going to start dealing with a lost man and then the devil is going to kill him before God can finish His work?

But sometimes the need to return to the church and tally a soul winning "score" up is far more pressing to a hyper-soul winner than actually letting God deal deeply with a lost sinner and bring forth a thorough conversion. We've got to count our scalps!

8. "Tonight my message will be on the importance of salvation . . . again."

As an evangelist I am sometimes without a meeting on a Sunday in a strange town. In that case my family and I look for an independent, Bible believing church to attend. On one such occasion I, my wife and our three sons walked into just such a church one Sunday morning. Now the **fact** is, that when we walk in there is little doubt as to our salvation. We come in wearing suits and ties while my wife has on a nice dress. We carry well worn Bibles and "Amen" the preacher when he nails a point down. On this particular morning we were the **only** visitors. The pastor preached a salvation message imploring the lost (wherever they were) to come forward and trust Christ. Okay, okay. I figured he geared his message to the chance that a lost person might have been brought in by a member. Evening services tend to be more "church family" oriented. Tonight he'll "feed the sheep." At the end of the service he announced the subject of his evening message. "Tonight my message will be on the importance of salvation." We left and found a different church to attend in hopes of getting preached to.

Many pastors boast of preaching, "The whole council of God." But to listen to them you realize that "The whole council of God" is "soul winning, soul winning, soul winning" and "Touch not God's anointed!"

Many pastors have been heard to actually brag, "My church is a spiritual maternity ward." And it's true! Their church is filled with spiritual babies. There is never any spiritual growth because the pastor never does anything but deliver babies. He doesn't feed his charges enough spiritual meat to cause them to grow up spiritually.

Why is this? That's simple. Many pastors don't **teach** the Bible because they don't **know** the Bible. Why is that? That's simple. They don't **know** the Bible because **they've been to "Bible" college!** Why didn't their "Bible" college education help them? Because most of their professors **didn't know the Bible.**

Why didn't their "Bible" college education help them? Because most of their professors **didn't know the Bible.**

Most "Bible" colleges offer fearless courses in "the Baptist distinctives", soul winning, the importance of the local church...and of course, the need for their graduates to remain ever loyal to their "Alma Mater." Beyond that it is a "milk bath." What's worse is that the graduate is never taught to read his Bible and study it independent of his "Virgin Mother." (**That's** what "Alma Mater" means! See. You went to Bible college and didn't even learn **that**!) Furthermore, a lazy graduate sees Bible study as boring and even dangerous. God forbid that his **personal** study reveal that, just maybe, his college was wrong in some area. He realizes that if he dares to waver from anything that he was taught he will hurt his standing with the "Alumni association." Neither God nor His Book are considered worth **that**. So, he becomes a fervent (and safe) soul winner. He preaches the need, the necessity, the command to win souls. He condemns anyone who isn't winning souls regularly and then, in his blind zeal, destroys any chance of anyone in his church ever growing by dogmatically claiming that "Soul winning is the **main theme** of the Bible." He has now doomed his people to spiritual ignorance. They will ever remain "children having children." And if anyone gets into their Bible and looks to grow beyond their pastor he'll personally kill them.

9. The death of Evangelism

With this shallow approach to Scripture has come the death of biblical evangelism. I am an evangelist. A **biblical** evangelist. (With no connection to the Bible rejecting paper of the same name.) We have no home. My family and I travel the country in a three year long circuit. Eighteen months in the East and eighteen months in the West. We pull a trailer and are in a different church every week.

In the last five decades the evangelist has been stereotyped as coming to town and having hundreds saved. **"That's what evangelism is!"** respond most

Christians. But that **is not** what **the Bible** says is the ministry of an evangelist. Ephesians, chapter four, enlightens us to the **biblical definition** of an evangelist.

Ephesians 4:11,12

11 *And he gave some, apostles; and some, prophets; and some, evangelists; and some, pastors and teachers;*

12 *For the **perfecting of the saints**, for the **work of the ministry**, for the **edifying of the body of Christ**:*

Notice that the three missions of the evangelist are **the same as the pastor**. Pastors and evangelists are both mentioned in the same verse and are told to :

1. perfect the **saints**

2. carry out the work of the ministry ("Ministry" is a term used in connection with the church.)

3. edify the body of Christ

None of these are interactive with the lost world. In fact, it is plain that the main assignment of the local church is to build up the saints, not be a "Spiritual Maternity Ward." My calling is to edify the saints in a local church...**just like the pastor**. The difference is that **I** do it for only one week in the year and the pastor's charge is to do it every Sunday.

But today no evangelist is considered successful if he can't report hundreds of conversions in every meeting. What has happened?

A simple degeneration in the call has taken place:

1. Evangelists had their faith in the infallibility of the Bible damaged by a critical college education.

2. Because they no longer trusted the Bible to be accurate, they quit reading it.

3. Since they were no longer reading their Bible, they were no longer getting anything from Scripture with which to "edify the body of Christ."

4. So how do they prove that God is still in their ministry? Simple. They do the same thing any two teenagers can do without a manual of operation...**they reproduce**.

5. Now they make spiritual reproduction **the main theme** of the Bible. So they can now claim that by winning souls they are doing the single most important thing God desires.

6. The biblical ministry of the evangelist is left dormant.

This mutation of the biblical evangelist has left our churches void of any real, meaty Bible teaching and replaced it with soul winning.

This mutation of the biblical evangelist has left our churches void of any real, meaty Bible teaching and replaced it with soul winning. One might ask, "Well if the lost don't get saved in **church**, just how are they going to get saved?" Simple. They will be lead to Christ **out in the field** by Christians who have been perfected and strengthened by the stout Bible teaching found in their church. Just like God intended!

This mutation has left us with an unreliable gauge by which to measure the success of **any** preacher, not just the evangelist. Success can only be gauged by how many "babies" were born. So what "soul winning equivalent" do we put on the value of a saved **marriage**? How do we assess the value of a sermon that persuades a Christian **not to commit**

suicide? What about a believer who is stopped short of committing adultery due to a message on the subject.[2]

But they have **no practical value** to the hyper-soul winner because there is no way to tally a figure for bragging rights. No preacher is ever asked, "How many marriages did you reclaim last week?" What pastor is going to stand up at a meeting of preachers and proclaim, "We had one saved, two marriages reclaimed, a brother who turned away from suicide and a woman who straightened up morally before she committed adultery." Every preacher in the place would be astounded by such a testimony. Then they would feel threatened because their ministry isn't producing the same results. Then one of them would self-righteously get up and demand that they get their attention back where it belongs, on soul winning.

10. Lost! The power of TRUTH

There is something unstoppable about Truth. It always touches a heart. Because we have replaced preaching with soul winning in our churches we have lost all confidence in the power that Truth has to get whatever spiritual job done that needs done. We can't imagine someone responding to a some spiritual need

2 None of these scenarios are hypothetical. I have heard them from people time and time again.

in their life if it hasn't been specifically mentioned in the sermon. Look! If you can get the Holy Spirit in your service He will accomplish whatever He wants, even if it hasn't been specifically mentioned from the pulpit. Two examples:

I have for years promoted Bible reading among the congregations where I preach. I suggest that every Christian read a Proverb for the day's date while they also start at the beginning of their Bible and read through it cover-to-cover at the rate of ten pages per day. In a revival meeting in Michigan I preached a message on that subject. It is geared directly to Christians. There is no gospel presentation in it. (Horrors!) At the end of the service **three people came forward and got saved!**

Once in Montana I was teaching, not preaching, but teaching on the corruptions of modern translations. I drew a chart and had several translations read aloud. We laughed at some of the foolish things found in so-called "improvements" on the King James. I pointed out some Roman Catholic based changes in the texts of some perversions. In the congregation that night was a lost, Roman Catholic woman. (Yes, I knew it. I **never** tried to insult her. I just didn't withhold Truth.) Obviously there was no gospel presentation. Yet at the end of the service she came forward and got saved. What did it? **The power of Truth!**

Some preachers defiantly boast, “Bless God. I don’t ever preach without a gospel presentation.” If you would just **truly** preach “the whole counsel of God” you might be surprised by what the Holy Spirit got done in your service

Again let me say it. Soul winning is important. Soul winning is very important. It simply isn’t **the main theme of the Bible**. And if it isn’t, what is?

CHAPTER TWO

For His Pleasure

Why are We Here?

That question has puzzled more than just a bunch of furry-headed philosophers. More than one Christian has wondered just what God put them on the earth to accomplish. The answer is found in what I call "The most important verse in the Bible." Why do I think it is the most important verse? If **just one single verse** can tell you why you're here and what you're supposed to be doing for the Lord for your whole life it is definitely the most important verse in the Bible. For the answer to why we are here, we are not at the mercy of anyone's prejudice. ("Soul winning, soul winning soul winning!") Nor do we need fear being victimized by some loosely wrapped philosophy. ("Go make the world a better place.")

To get to the most important verse in the Bible you have to read all the way through it. Just as you near the end you will stumble upon Revelation 4:11:

Thou art worthy, O Lord, to receive glory and honour and power: for thou hast created all things, and ***for thy pleasure*** *they are and were created.*

In that short declaration of praise, shouted to God by the twenty-four elders in Heaven, we find the reason for our existence. **We were put here to be a PLEASURE to our Creator.**

This is one hundred and eighty degrees out from what is commonly accepted in the mind of man. We have the mistaken idea that **God** exists for **our pleasure**. When in fact the exact opposite is true. You say **you're** different? Let's check. Review your prayers of the last week and see how many times they consisted of what **God could do to make you happy** rather than the other way around. We are here to put a smile on God's face. How many times have you started your day by asking, "Lord, what can I do to put a smile on **Your** face today?"

We were put here to be a Pleasure to our Creator.

Your petty successes mean nothing if you haven't lived in such a way as to put a smile on the face of your Creator. Now really, did you think He was going to be impressed by your softball trophy? Your ten-point buck? Your beautiful livingroom decor?

This is the problem with the "Soul winning, soul winning, soul winning!" philosophy. The entire focus is one hundred and eighty degrees out from what it should be. Examples?

1. Soul winners are motivated by the need to keep people out of Hell. They think of the **human** consequence of rejecting Christ. Rather they should be motivated by the desire to see someone get saved so that they will **finally** be in the position to do what they were created to do. Glorify God.

2. Because the emphasis of the "Soul winning, soul winning, soul winning!" crowd is only to "get souls saved" they see the salvation of a sinner as **an end** rather than **a beginning**. Remember: **birth** is a **beginning** not an end. Being "born again" is the **beginning** of one's **real** life. Not the end.

3. Once a hyper-soul winner wins someone to Christ they head for the next door at a run and never look back. A newborn baby is left to fend for itself.

4. Hyper-soul winning churches are geared to leading people to Christ but totally unprepared to **raise** the new convert. (Except to teach them how to soul win.) We all have the same complaint about welfare mothers. They all know how to **have** children but they don't know how to **raise them**. Having a baby is a relatively short period of time in relationship to the length of a child's life. But **raising** them takes a **lifetime**. It requires teaching correct values, teaching a child to care for itself. Teaching it to say "No" to itself to keep out of trouble. It is a slow, day-after-day, week-after-week, month-after-month, year-after-year process that is not near as glamorous as carrying around a new baby every nine months.

Explaining Creation

Let's examine the three questions we sought answers for earlier. This time we will view them in the light of the **main** theme of the Bible being our being a pleasure to our Creator rather than "Soul winning, soul winning, soul winning!".

1. Why did He create the universe? To get pleasure from it.

2. Why did He make man? To get pleasure from him.

3. What does He want from us more than anything else? Pleasure.

It works! Being a pleasure to our Creator satisfies the questions of life. The fact of the matter is that God wants pleasure from the vilest of men. Now do you see, I mean **really** see, what is wrong with the Howard Sterns and Larry Flynts of this world? They are not being a pleasure to the God that created them.

And yet they are no more a failure than is a carnal Christian.

Babies are Cute, Adults can be Ugly

Have you ever thought about this? (Have you ever thought?) There was a time when Adolf Hitler was a cute little baby. He was, no doubt, the joy of his parents. He cooed and giggled and caused people to say, "Isn't he adorable?" Yet look what he was when he grew up. A cold-blooded murderer.

It is easy to look at the birth of a baby as a wonderful thing. That's because it is. But it is **not** a "success story." When the child has grown up, stayed true to the Lord, kept out of trouble, never broken his parents' heart, **that** is a success story.

It is just as easy to see the salvation of a soul as a wonderful thing. It is. But **it is not a "success story."** When the new convert has grown spiritually, purged his life of undesirable practices and stayed in church for life, **that's** a "success story." But what pastor can or will brag about that?

From the moment a child is born there is a predetermined state sometime in it's future when it will lean towards self-destruction. We call it "teenager."Someone who was a "cute" baby may, fifteen or sixteen years later take dope, have an illegitimate child or kill somebody. You see, **birth** was not the final say on their existence. Somewhere during the raising process something was left out. We have all seen spoiled children throwing a tantrum in a store as their powerless parents whimpered in protest. Gee, but they **were** a cute baby. Weren't they? **And it doesn't even matter!**

God has placed a great institution on earth to help properly raise them and guide them in the right direction. It's called "parenthood."

Babies are cute, but they are gross. They burp out loud. They throw up on themselves and others. They cry when they don't get their way. And they do terrible things to their drawers. All of which is acceptable for two reasons. One, they're just a baby. Two, in spite of all this, they're still cute. But they don't stay a baby forever. And they certainly outgrow the "cute" stage. They had better have learned to control themselves by this time or no one's going to want to sit next to them in church! But God has placed a great institution on earth to help properly raise them and guide them in the right direction. It's called "parenthood." God has placed parents on this earth to correctly raise children. If all they do is have children but do not properly raise them then the children will remain immature in intellect even though they grow physically.

A newborn Christian is also "cute." Especially if they have no knowledge of Christianity. They will say funny things. They will happily embarrass themselves and others. And sometimes they will cry when they don't get their way. But God has placed a great institution on this earth to properly raise newborn babes in Christ. It's called the "Local Church." God has placed local churches on this earth to correctly raise spiritual babies. If all a church does is have babies but does not properly raise them then those spiritual babies will remain immature in spirit even though they spend years in church. Although their spiritual "birth" took only seconds, their spiritual **maturity** may take years.

How to be a Pleasure to Your Creator

If you are a parent, think back to what was a delight to you as your children grew up. They first learned to care for themselves, tying their own shoes, dressing themselves, cleaning their room. Then you began to educate them. They learned to read, reason and make decisions. Soon they got a job and started producing as well as earning an income. And what parent didn't love it when they asked advice or did something just to please their parents. My sons still think to pick any wild flowers they see to give to their mother.

If a child grows physically but not mentally we say that his mental growth has been retarded. At age one he may cry when he doesn't get his way. But he can do no more because he has no strength. But by the time he's forty, with a one year old's intellect he is going to be a force to reckon with. Now he will **hurt you** if he doesn't get his way.

So how can we please our Creator? Well, we start by growing spiritually. That comes from the input of the Bible. And that input occurs in two ways.

So how can we please our Creator? Well, we start by growing spiritually.

Through daily reading and through submitting ourselves to the preaching of our local church. That is why I teach that we should read a minimum of ten pages everyday. Let a goodly portion of the Word enter your heart and mind and begin to bring about slow but steady changes. I also preach that you should be in church every time the doors are open. Preaching will give the Holy Spirit a chance to influence your life as nothing else can. (That's why people are quick to use feeble excuses to drop out of church. It's called avoiding conviction.)

So lets take a typical, worldly young man who gets saved around the age of twenty-one. All right, so he has now avoided Hell. That's wonderful. But he needs to start growing spiritually or be doomed to being spiritually retarded. Our young convert comes to church and somewhere along the line hears that it is a shame for a man to have long hair. He resists the thought of cutting his hair but has been taught to submit to Scripture. He goes to the barber and shows up the next Sunday with a decent hair cut. **He** is growing...and **God is smiling!**

Next he realizes that he should dress his best for the Lord. He quits coming to church in shabby clothes and buys a white shirt and tie. And God smiles. Then one day at work he is convicted that his "Budweiser" shirt shouldn't be worn by one of God's children. He makes the change. He changes his language, his jokes, what he does to pass the time. One day he hears that one tenth of what he owns is already God's so he starts tithing. Can you imagine the **joy** each one of these changes brings to his heavenly Father?

Now, years have gone by. He's long been a deacon in his church. He teaches Sunday school class for beginner boys. He has grown. One day his job takes him out of town. He goes to a newsstand to buy a paper and a pornographic magazine catches his eye. "Hmm? Absolutely no one would ever know. I mean, it's not like I'm going out on my wife. It will just be once." What does he do? Well, he either makes God smile or frown. Either way no one may ever know about his small personal battle. But **God** will. Can you see the tremendous opportunity to put a smile on God's face. Forget the threats that, "You'll get caught!" The **fact** is that you might not. But **God** will still lose.

Suppressing the Flesh

The greatest single enemy a Christian has is **not** the devil. It is **his own flesh**. If the devil died tomorrow there would still be Christians falling into sin due to the power their flesh holds in their lives. Add to that the fact that we won't get new flesh until the Lord comes back for us. (Phil 3:21) Wonderful! But a little too late to help us in the battles of life. But God has not left us without help. He has given us a Book. A Book that possesses both a spiritual nature and spiritual power. Reading this Book is the greatest single help there is to suppressing the flesh. As the words of this Book enter the eye they begin to

If the devil died tomorrow there would still be Christians falling into sin due to the power their flesh holds in their lives.

strengthen us **against** our flesh. We cannot eliminate our old nature, but we can **suppress it**. And that is what needs to be done. Our tempers, our lusts, our malice, our doubts, our fears, all are products of our flesh which can destroy us. Reading the Bible helps us to control our flesh.

Preaching is the other method for suppressing our innate wickedness. Bible reading is something we do everyday. Preaching is something we only experience on a weekly basis. In spite of our Bible reading we may still retain some ungodly influences in our lives. That's because our hearts are wicked so we resist what the Bible has shown us. To sit under preaching is to put oneself smack in the center of a spiritual bull's eye, with the Holy Spirit taking the shots. You need it. But if the preaching is nothing more than salvation message after salvation message your heart will never be dealt with. You will never come under Holy Spirit conviction and you will never change your wicked actions in an effort to be a pleasure to your Creator. (Except for your horrible sin of not winning enough souls.)

The immorality that is too common among some of the "Soul winning, soul winning, soul winning!" crowd would be suppressed and eliminated it they believed that their **main** goal in life should be to be a pleasure to God rather than simply win souls. Preacher! Don't violate your calling by using it for an occasion for your flesh to indulge itself. Every preacher has such an opportunity at some point. Forget about the threat of getting caught. Forget about the consequences. Think about the failure to be a pleasure to your Maker!

The WHOLE "Whole Council of God"

With the understanding that we are to be a pleasure to our Creator we can see the immense opening to preaching that is available. Our pulpits aren't just weapons to be used to herd our people into doing no more than win souls and tithe. Suddenly the importance of simply **telling the truth** becomes not only important, but a necessary subject for a sermon. Cleanliness, child rearing, the timely paying of debts, not taking God's name in vain: all become imperative for a pastor to convey to his congregation.

Beyond that, the proper "raising of one of God's babies" will require the teaching of doctrine. Doctrine is designed to separate the believer from false teaching. Eternal security, baptism, the deity of Christ, the infallibility of Scripture are just a few of the truths that should thunder from our pulpits.

We also begin to see the need to delve into the deeper things of Scripture. Every believer fully realizes that the Bible is much deeper than the mere words on the page. One of the things that really immerses a Christian in their Bible is to see the veiled things made plain.
* Who were the "sons of God" of Genesis chapter six?
* Where are the Scripture to substantiate your answer?
* What was Lucifer's "job description" in eternity past prior to his fall?
* When did that fall happen?
* What did those two loaves that Saul was given in 1 Samuel, chapter ten, represent, and why was one loaf withheld from him?

Not important you say? Those questions are just as important as how a pencil sharpener works, or how a caterpillar changes into a butterfly or any of the other seemingly unimportant questions a child asks.

Without delving into the Bible our life will be filled with unanswered questions. Questions whose answers lay dormantly waiting the reader in an unread Bible.

Why is there a dearth of Bible preaching in our Churches?

Most public schools have become nothing but institutions used to indoctrinate our children in socialism and humanism. Teachers seem bent on taking every opportunity to steer their young scholars to the need for more "one world" thinking. Believe it or not this is not all done with a sinister spirit.

Most public schools have become nothing but institutions used to indoctrinate our children in socialism and humanism.

Although some teachers teach such damnable things because they are agents of a lower power, most do it for a more benign reason. **They don't know anything else.** Look, our schools have "dumbed down" their student bodies for decades now. Then these graduates go on college to be teachers and learn **absolutely**

nothing from the college professors. Having learned no "cold, hard facts" in college they are faced with a dilemma when they command their first class. **They don't know the subject they're supposed to be teaching!** So they do the only thing they can. They **fake** their way through the school year emphasizing to their victims the importance of environmentalism, socialism, "freedom" of sexual choice and so on. They simply **don't know anything but theory**.

Many pastors, unfortunately, graduate from "Bible" college no better equipped than their secular counterparts. They know no more Bible than the shallow experience of their "New Testament Survey" class. They certainly cannot teach what they do not know so they fall back to the only thing they can...soul winning. Or, they **could** spend hours studying their Bibles and make up for the deficiency of their education. But then what happens if they find out that everything they were taught wasn't correct? If they waver from the "party line" of their "Alma Mater" they stand a chance of being ostracized by the alumni. Nope, feeding a few babies isn't worth it. So they take the plunge and declare that soul winning is not only important, but that it is the absolutely, singly **most important** thing that God wants them to do. Forget Revelation 4:11. They didn't know it was in there anyway. Now they and their church are doomed to a future of Bible ignorance as they watch baby after baby delivered and try to convince themselves that all this crying and all these dirty diapers are the will of God.

CHAPTER THREE

God vs. Man

There is a subtle but errant foundation upon which the "Soul winning, soul winning, soul winning!" philosophy is built. It emphasizes **Man** more than **God.** This undercurrent is almost invisible due to the hype made of "the value of one soul." Yet this very tenet is the "all and everything" of the hyper-soul winning movement.

Man is bad. He is born bad and goes downhill from there. Some of his innate error is easy to see. His thirst for sinful pleasure is as hard to recognize as the lights of downtown Las Vegas. Every Christian recognizes the wickedness of the human heart and is quick to avoid being caught up in it. Yet **some** of Man's waywardness is harder to discern. Man is innately selfish. Some of his selfishness is easily discernable. Some is far more subtle. It is this **subtle** selfishness that we will deal with here.

Basically Man wants to always put himself first. He cuts you off in traffic, bucks in line, promotes his own personal agenda and generally does this in complete ignorance of the shallowness of his actions. Most Christians recognize this overt trait in man and attempt to curtail it in themselves. But it is still present, none the less. This subtle selfishness is nowhere more evident than in the "Soul winning, soul winning, soul winning!" philosophy. Think! Why are we ever hounded and harangued to win souls? "Because they're going to **Hell!**" But it's more than that. It's because **they're** going to Hell!

Soul winners are constantly reminding everyone that will listen about the fate of the lost. Then they mix in a little guilt and intimidation to arrive at the misguided conclusion that, "Soul winning is the main theme of the Bible." When they deal with a lost soul they are there to save him from Hell. They are there to save him from God's judgement. But wait! If they are there to save him from God's judgement then they are there to save him from **God.** God plans on putting every sinner who rejects Christ in Hell. Suddenly we find the soul winner alluding to this judgement and, in fact, making God the **villain** of the situation. They are there to save the lost from what **God** has planned for them. It's basically, "Look, Pal, **God** is going to put you in Hell but **I'm** here to save you from Him."

Today's soul winning deals with the lost man in only two ways:

1. If you **don't** get saved look what you face.
2. If you **do** get saved look what you get.

What **God** gets or doesn't get isn't even in the equation. No one is interested in **God** benefitting from any of this. Oh, sure, the ever resilient soul winner will spout, "God wants people saved. So I'm pleasing Him by leading lost souls to Christ." That is nothing more than someone trying to twist and wedge their priority to fit a description of God's.

An Invalid Prayer

I was raised Roman Catholic. Immediately after I trusted Christ I labored under the same two false assumptions that most new converts do: **1.** I thought my friends and family **had not heard** the Gospel. **2.** I **thought they'd be excited** when I told it to them. Whoa! Was that ever a pipedream! But regardless of

---

But in my sincerity and ignorance I didn't know that **it was an invalid prayer.**

---

the opposition and disinterest I faithfully witnessed to my family, on one occasion even taking Dr. John R.

Rice by to try to win my father to Christ. It was all to no avail. They were not interested. My parents had heard the Gospel for years, even before I was born, and they rejected God's gift of eternal life.

Years came and went and I continued my spiritual plowing, watering and whatever else I could call it. Like most sincere Christians who love their parents, I prayed for my mother and father to get saved. My prayer was basically, "Lord, please save my Dad and Mom **because I love them** and don't want to see them go to Hell." I prayed this prayer consistently. I prayed this prayer fervently. Many times I prayed this prayer with tears streaming down my face. But in my sincerity and ignorance I didn't know that **it was an invalid prayer.** "What?" You say. How could praying for the salvation of someone you love be an invalid prayer. I was not wrong for praying for my parents. I was wrong in the manner in which I did it, and that's what made my prayer invalid.

I was trained as were most Christians to think of nothing but, "Souls burning in Hell" when I witnessed. I was there to stop that. I was there to save them from Hell and God's judgement. I was there **for them**, not God. I wasn't the least bit interested in how **God** might benefit from my parents' conversion. I just didn't want them to go to Hell and burn for eternity. This is what motivates soul winning today. In fact, Christians are browbeaten and intimidated for not "caring enough about the lost." Today in our churches grown men stand behind our pulpits and conjure up crocodile tears to prove that they "love" every soul and simply can't stand the thought of even one person going to Hell. This is **bunk**. **Nobody** loves **everybody**.

"Others!" is the same cry used by UNICEF, the United Nations, NATO, the heart fund and the AIDS coalition.

This "putting man first" philosophy has been so ingrained into the hearers in our churches and Bible colleges that to not subscribe to it borders on heresy. "Others!" is the cry that is heard from pulpits around our country. Of course, "Others!" is also the same cry used by UNICEF, the United Nations, NATO, the heart fund, the AIDS coalition and every other one-world organization. Somehow our goal of pleasing God has been redirected into a goal of accommodating Man. Who cares what God gets, we kept another of our fellow **humans** out of Hell. This approach makes Man the most important individual in the Bible rather than God. The soul winner then becomes a servant of Man rather than God. Man's pleasure is our greatest goal rather than God's. **It's all backwards!**

A Valid Prayer

I pondered this selfish element of my burden for my parents and the resulting prayer and decided to change it. I ceased praying, "Lord, please save my Dad and Mom **because I love them** and don't want to see them go to Hell." I thought of His Son and the pain, shame and horror of the cross. I realized that the only thing that made it worth it to Him was the salvation of lost souls. I realized that, when a person dies without Christ they make what Jesus did **a vain act.** What He suffered was a **waste**. How would you feel if you had gone through what He did on the cross and then you saw people reject it and make it worthless? Then I realized that when someone trusts Christ they make His sacrifice worth it all. They validate His suffering. I began to pray, "Lord please continue to deal with my parents about their lost condition. For if they get saved, it will make what Jesus experienced on the cross worth it. Furthermore, if they get saved they **will finally** be in a position to fulfill Revelation 4:11 and be a pleasure to You, their Creator." I can't guarantee that it was the change in my prayer, but on September 19, 1982 my parents came forward in the church that I was pastoring in Auburn, New York and trusted Christ.[3] Did God get anything from their salvation? Yes. My father, who had always "cussed like a sailor" **immediately** (I mean, **that night!**) stopped cussing and I never heard him take God's name in vain again for the remaining ten years of his life. Don't you think God was pleased by that?

We need to overcome our innate selfishness and quit seeing only the benefit that salvation brings to Man. We need to look at soul winning as an opportunity to place someone in a position where they can finally fulfill Revelation 4:11 rather than nothing more than a divine fire escape from Hell. Remember! We call it, Being "**born again**." It's a **beginning** not an ending.

We need to quit trying to exalt the position of Man in Scripture. We need to quit attempting to make him the most important character in the Bible. **God**

---

3 I certainly don't claim that such a prayer will **guarantee** the salvation of the person you're praying for, but it **certainly** will make their salvation of **personal** interest to God. I mentioned this change in my prayer in a message I preached in a church in Montana. Four weeks later a woman came up to me in another church and mentioned that she had been there and heard that point and that she had begun praying for her lost daughter's salvation so that **God** would get something from it after that service. She told me, "Two weeks later my daughter got saved!"

does not exist for **our** pleasure. **We** exist for **His** pleasure! We shouldn't be winning people to Christ because of the benefit to **them**. We shouldn't be winning people to Christ because of the joy their conversion brings to **us**. We should be winning them because of the benefit their salvation is to **God**. For **GOD** is the most important character in Scripture. **God** is the reason we exist. We should be more afraid of failing to please God than the thought of all the lost souls in the world going to Hell.

CHAPTER FOUR

Growth vs. Birth

A Beginning is Just a Beginning

As stated earlier, everyone likes babies. They giggle and coo and are generally as cute as they are harmless. Everyone wants to see a newborn baby. A household is blessed by the regular addition of such lovable creatures. But what happens if they never grow up? Every grandparent will tell you that they love **holding** their grandchildren but they are glad when the time comes that they can give them back to their parents. Furthermore, there is a great, undeserved and unappreciated burden for any grandparent who is forced to raise their grandchildren because of the irresponsibility of the children's parents. "We just can't take the crying like we used to," they say.

Imagine for a moment that two young people get married. One day, after the appointed time they have a baby. The child is normal and healthy and **cute**. The young parents are thrilled. After awhile another child is born to them. And another. Each one is cute in its own way. Eight, nine, **ten** come their way from

God. But there is a problem. None of them grow up. They all stop growing around their first or second year. Soon the house is full of dirty diapers, temper tantrums, fights and crying that never stops. You can only imagine the frustration of the young parents. Babies are cute. But babies that stay babies **are not**.

The "Soul winning, soul winning, soul winning!" philosophy teaches that there is nothing more important than "having babies". The greatest good a person can do is to win a soul. After all, what could be more noble than saving a soul from an eternity in a lake of fire? And what greater blessing is there to a church than having one more spiritual newborn around the place? But, just like real babies, spiritual babies don't stay cute forever. A church full of spiritual babies is soon a church full of snobbery, infighting, **out**-fighting, complaining and just about any other action a spoiled little child is capable of. Although birth is exciting and refreshing, eternal childhood is a grievous burden to all affected by it.

Many pastors, seeing the immaturity of their congregation, but damning those same congregations to just such actions by their shallow preaching, are forced to resort to strong arm tactics. A man in the congregation becomes a threat to his pastor when he becomes more spiritual than him. (Or when he **thinks** he is.) If you have a shallow pastor who never studies his Bible, he is someday going to be passed up by some avid young baby who is beginning to really get into his Bible. Sooner or later he's going to show up at his pastor's office to ask about a discrepancy between what he sees plainly in his Bible and some fantasy of his pastor's preaching. The pastor, not really upset by the man but **quite** threatened by the fact that the young man seems to be correct in his assumption, feels he needs to cover his biblical ignorance. There is no greater method than, "I'm God's anointed! Don't you ever come in here and question me!" Thus, the only baby who was beginning to grow had to be killed lest he surpass (and threaten) his pastor.

How NOT to do it

To the shallow or lazy pastor there is one fool-proof way to con the congregation into thinking they are a student of the Bible. It consists of two magic words; "The Greek."

Study of "the Greek" is the laziest method there is to pretending to be a Bible student. **Greek** study is not **Bible** study. You can study Greek without ever having a Bible in the same room. Greek study is the "Holy Grail" of lazy, egotistical preachers. It has everything needed to dazzle the church folks and cover up the biblical ignorance of the pastor:

1. It is a foreign language. **Everybody** is impressed with someone who knows a foreign language. "Look how many years he's studied that there Greek. He sur are edgicated. He must be a expurt!"

2. Because Greek **is** a foreign language, and **biblical** Greek is even different than modern Greek, the preacher need not worry about someone coming up and saying, "Your declension of that verb was improper." Basically his listeners will simply say, "It's all Greek to me."

3. Greek exposition is completely subjective. In other words, there's no "wrong" change you can make

Study of "the Greek" is the laziest method there is to pretending to be a Bible student. Greek study is not Bible study.

to a text. I have taught for years a lesson I call "The Greek Game." It has only one rule. "The King James Bible is **always** wrong." So, if a given Greek word could have been translated any one of seven ways, all the lazy preacher needs to do is pick one of the other six and expound on its virtues. **Any** one of the other six. It doesn't matter as long as you're showing people how smart you are by being able to correct God's choice.[4]

4. Best of all, **you don't need to know Greek to use it!** There are ample "helps" which will help the ministerial con-man to hoodwink the fools in the pews into thinking he is highly educated.[5]

It does not matter how sincere or desirous to learn a preacher may seem. Use of the Greek constitutes a veiled attack on the credibility of Scripture. The preacher makes himself look good **at the expense of the Bible**. And worst of all, he **still** doesn't know his Bible any better than he did before his foray into the nether world of "Greek scholarship." But it is much easier than actual **study** of the Scripture.

---

4 I once heard two different preachers change the very same word in the very same verse in two different sermons twenty-four hours apart. Both changed God's choice to a different word but neither agreed with the other as to what the proper translations should be. But that's okay. They **both** agreed that **the King James Bible was wrong**. That's all that mattered. Their respective congregations were impressed at their "great intellect."

5 I heard a **fourteen**-year-old boy during a "Preaching Contest" correct the Bible using the magical Greek. He didn't know Greek. He just knew the rule and knew how to use the "helps" supplied by greedy book stores to his advantage.

Using Time and Energy Wisely

If a biblical novice wants to learn his Bible he needs to begin by praying. I don't mean a sanctimonious prayer. I mean a desperate prayer begging God to unlock the words of His Book so that he will be able to better feed His flock. God is the author of Scripture and if He locks the door no amount of Greek or anything else is going to budge it. Furthermore, if there is secret sin in the life of the preacher he can forget any light from God. Why should a holy God reveal anything to a hypocrite? He'd better go back to "the Greek." He can always get a "nugget" there without the need of God's help.

The sincere preacher needs to realize that he is going to have to spend many hours in true study of the Bible rather than wasting his time playing computer games.

There are helps that can be used. A concordance is helpful. Today we have electric Bibles and computer Bible programs that can help a student find a verse or a particular word. (But beware of the commentaries that refer you to "the Greek." A Bible atlas is also helpful.

Halley's Bible Handbook is a treasure house of information while *Larkin's Dispensational Truth* will help to explain seemingly contradictory passages. The sincere preacher needs to realize that he is going to have to spend many hours in true study of the Bible rather than wasting his time playing computer games. (This may hamper perfecting your golf game but your sheep will grow better.)

Signs of Growth

There are several ways to check on your spiritual growth. Two of them are simple checklists found within the pages of the Bible itself. You would do well to check your spiritual growth against God's word rather than some preachers opinion. Checking yourself over the **years** against these lists will help you determine how well your spiritual maturity is coming along.

Check List # 1

1. Romans 5:3-5

3 *And not only so, but we glory in tribulations also: knowing that tribulation worketh patience;*

4 *And patience, experience; and experience, hope:*

5 *And hope maketh not ashamed; because the love of God is shed abroad in our hearts by the Holy Ghost which is given unto us.*

In these three verses we see four phases of Christian growth:

1. Tribulation
2. Patience
3. Experience
4. Hope

1. Tribulation - The process is easy to follow. Children always react more radically to things that upset or scare them than do adults. Why? Because adults have "been there before." A young Christian is likely to panic due to the introduction of **tribulation** into their life. They have never experienced the pressure or grief associated with disasters and problems. It may be that they thought that having trusted Christ would keep such things from ever afflicting them again. But there is definitely a desire to run and hide. But if the young Christian will "run and hide" in their **Bible** and **refuse** to drop out of church or get mad at God they will ever so slowly begin to develop **patience**.

2. Patience - Tribulation makes one want to panic. If **patience** is anything it is the absence of panic. What would have greatly upset a newborn babe in Christ, if it had happened the first year after he got saved, should be greeted with much less agitation when it occurs nine or ten years after their salvation.

Why? Because previous **tribulation** has worked **patience** into their life.

3. Experience - As the Christian matures they will begin to view each new problem in their life with less and less emotion. Why? **Experience.** Just as "Been there. Done that." can take the excitement out of life it can also eliminate the emotional highs and lows akin to immaturity.

4. Hope - Finally, after a number of decades, the Christian will be faced with what would have seemed insurmountable twenty years earlier. Now, not only will they not panic, but a wry smile will come across their face. Why? Because they have seen God pull them out of so many messes before this that they realize **they're going to get to see God work!** It's called **hope**. You don't automatically get it along with your salvation. You don't get it the first time you experience tribulation. It takes years of sticking with the Lord to **grow up** enough to reach this point of quiet confidence.

But if you let the tribulation of the early years cause you to drop out of church, close your Bible and quit on God, you have lost the battle completely. **Don't quit!**

Check List #2

2. 2 Peter 1:5-8

5 *And beside this, giving all diligence, add to your faith virtue; and to virtue knowledge;*

6 *And to knowledge temperance; and to temperance patience; and to patience godliness;*

7 *And to godliness brotherly kindness; and to brotherly kindness charity.*

8 *For if these things be in you, and abound, they make you that ye shall neither be barren nor unfruitful in the knowledge of our Lord Jesus Christ.*

The first chapter of 2 Peter contains a tremendous look at the progressive growth of a young Christian:

1. Faith
2. Virtue
3. Knowledge
4. Temperance
5. Patience
6. Godliness
7. Brotherly kindness
8. Charity

1. Faith - Faith is the starting point. It refers to your salvation. It is your spiritual beginning. It's when you were "born again." It's wonderful but it produces nothing more than an uninitiated baby. There are years of growth ahead.

2. Virtue - Virtue is associated with such words as; chastity, chivalry, goodness, morality, virginity, honor, integrity, purity and sanctity. (In other words, they are in **no way** associated with the name: Bill Clinton.) It might also be noted that these are words not associated with the world. Higher education has been described in many ways but never with any of the above words. Young people being saved out of the rock culture are almost completely void of these attributes.

Virtue is directly connected to the strength we need to overcome the trials and temptations of life.

Virtue is directly connected to the **strength** we need to overcome the trials and temptations of life. Once virtue is lost there is a degree of spiritual weakness that will effect the Christian in every battle of life.

Suddenly we begin to see why it is imperative to teach moral purity from our pulpits. Is a generation void of morality going to enter our congregations and all we're going to do is **tell them to win souls?!** They have no concept of purity. They need to be instructed in it **by someone who is pure**!

But there is an even deeper spiritual value to virtue. One that may decide the fate of a young Christian years before they finally succumb due to its absence. There is a mystique about virtue. There is a power in purity that cannot be obtained in any other way. The *Oxford English Dictionary* declares that virtue is: "The power or operative influence inherent in a supernatural or divine being."

Do you remember the comment of the Lord Jesus when the woman with the bloody issue secretly touched Him and was healed? He said that He knew **virtue** had gone out of Him.

We will get into situations in our lives that require the supernatural power that is only supplied by **virtue** to get through. If we have not purged our lives of uncleanness then we will be vexed by a spiritual weakness that cannot be overcome by methods or all the "help books" in the world. Purity is not a choice. It is a matter of our spiritual survival. How many have fallen because years earlier they had scoffed at the idea of living virtuously as just so much "legalism"?

3. Knowledge - Most assuredly this is not talking about **worldly** knowledge. How well you do calculus or what you know about fixing cars is not going to secure your life in Christ. It is plain that God expects us to apply ourselves to knowing His Book and by that knowing **Him**.

When you read a book you unconsciously "read the author". More than once I have had people who never met me but had read my books say that they felt like they already knew me when we met for the first time. This is normal. Having the Bible is a great advantage. Understanding the truth about the King James Bible being God's absolute word is even better. But remember: the Israelites had **the Ark** in 1 Samuel, chapter four, but they had no relationship with **the God of the Ark.** Too many King James Bible believers think that believing the King James Bible is the perfect Word of God gives them a spiritual advantage over other Christians. But they need **more** than the King James Bible. They need a relationship with **the God of the King James Bible**. We need to know God and there is no better way to get to know Him than by reading His Book over and over and over again. (Unless you're expecting Him to show up glowing in your bedroom some evening.)

Furthermore we need to remember that it is **that Book** that makes us different from the world. Therefore we need to have a knowledge of its truths. We need to be "people of the Book". We need to tie our lives inseparably to its words and teaching. This simply will not happen hearing messages on "Soul winning, soul winning, soul winning!" every week and spending our spare time water skiing.

4. Temperance - There is much said about "Balance" in today's churches. Not bad considering that the word never appears in Scripture! "Balance" isn't our goal. **Temperance** is.

We are people of extremes. We seem either to gorge ourselves or starve ourselves. Yet temperance is the answer. Honey is good for you. The psalmist stated that the words of God were sweeter than honey. (Ps. 119:103) In fact, the land that God promised to Israel could only be described as "a land flowing with milk and honey."

The problem with humans is this. We want all we can get of a good thing. We reason that if honey is good for us then we need to partake of as much honey as we can. It is known to be a blood purifier. The more honey we consume the heathier we will be. Someone needs to come out with the "Honey Only" diet. It is obviously the answer to all our health needs.

But, suddenly we read in Proverbs 25:16 that honey can make us sick. Ah! Then what we really need to do is to eliminate honey completely from our diets. It's dangerous. It could kill us. They ought to make it a "controlled substance."

Which view is correct? Neither. Honey **is** good for us. But the Bible says that **too much** can make you sick. What's the answer? Temperance. We should neither eliminate it nor subsist entirely on it. We should use it in moderation.

**"Balance" isn't our goal.
Temperance is.**

As the young child of God grows he should not be so reactionary to what he hears. Temperance teaches us not to be too quick to "jump on the wagon" but neither to be in a hurry to jump "off."

So we hear something unflattering (I said "unflattering". I didn't say "sin") about a fellow Christian. Then we should immediately break fellowship with them and then go further and separate from anyone else who doesn't break fellowship with them. Temperance will rather cause us not to be too quick to act and may save us some grief when we discover the problem wasn't as bad as we first heard.

Temperance in our lives will help us to better handle the good times as well as the bad times in our lives. It will keep us from getting too emotionally low when we're in a valley but it will throttle back our exuberance when we are on a spiritual mountain peak. Temperance is good. But it's not the first thing you get in your Christian life after faith. It comes years down the road. If it comes at all. If you weren't spending all your time soul winning.

5. Patience - Patience must be very important and very hard to attain because it the only attribute found in both lists, 2 Peter 1 and Romans 5. Romans five tells how we **get** patience. 2 Peter 1 tells us that it is an integral part of a mature Christian. An impatient Christian has a growth problem. Now wait a minute! Remember, patience comes **with time**. Don't read this and say to yourself, "That's just what old so-in-so's problem is!" Have a little patience. Will you?

6. Godliness - The word "godliness" refers to "God-likeness." If a person is "god-ly" they are "like-God" in the attributes of their personality. **That** is a tall order. So what are the attributes of God that we need in our lives? There are five prominent attributes of our God that appear over-and-over again throughout Scripture and which separate Him from the gods of the heathen. They are well defined in Jonah 4:2. When Jonah's anger was kindled because God spared Nineveh he complained of God's five attributes as though they were flaws.

Jonah 4:2 *And he prayed unto the LORD, and said, I pray thee, O LORD, was not this my saying, when I was yet in my country? Therefore I fled before unto Tarshish: for I knew that thou art a* ***gracious*** *God, and* ***merciful, slow to anger****, and of* ***great kindness,*** *and* ***repentest thee of the evil****.*

Now if there is anything a baby **isn't**, it's "gracious, merciful, slow to anger, of great kindness and repents of any evil." So if you find these attributes lacking in your character...**guess what you are?!**

a. Merciful - The difference between mercy and grace is this. "Mercy" is **not getting bad that you deserve**. Grace is **getting good that you don't deserve**. If you had died in a car wreck before you got saved and gone to Hell you would have gotten what you deserved. If you were spared, it **was not** the "grace" of God. It was the **mercy** of God.

So have you ever had anyone "dead to rights" and felt so much compassion for them that you withheld their **well deserved** punishment? I'm not talking about being bullied into accepting the sinful ways of an unrepentant person. But has there ever been someone that perhaps you didn't like and you were in a position to cause them great grief and you didn't? That's mercy. That's God-like.

b. Gracious - God's grace is best displayed in our lives in the free salvation he gives us through the death, burial and resurrection of His Son, Jesus Christ. But there have probably been many occasions when the Lord has been gracious to you in many ways since your salvation. (If you're not saved you need to trust Him as your own personal Saviour right now.)

Have you ever done something good for someone that they did not deserve and that you did not benefit from in some way? That's gracious. That's God-like.

c. Slow to Anger - (Should we go on to the next point instead?) Do you have a volatile temper? Are you so stupid that you're **proud** of it. Or do you excuse yourself by saying, "That's just me." Well that's **not** "just God." And it is **not** Godly.

d. Great Kindness - Kindness is found in those little things God does that wouldn't make any difference in your life if He didn't do them. They're just His way of saying, "I love you." Grace may be the answer to a prayer at a crucial time. But kindness is some little thing God passed your way. I call them "Tokens of Love" and they just put a smile on your face and sometimes a tear in your eye.

Have you ever, for no reason, simply done something just to show kindness to someone?

e. Repent of the Evil - Mercy is not doing something bad to someone that they deserve. Repenting of the evil is when you had already made your plans to do the bad act. It may be a secret sin on your part. It may be something gauged to cause harm to someone you don't like. It is still evil. Have you ever repented of such a thing? Or did you just run to the Bible and find a verse to justify your cruelty.

This fivefold list is found in Jonah 4:2, Nehemiah 9:17 and Joel 2:13. These attributes are what make our God different than the gods of the heathen. All the gods of the heathen are angry. **Our** God is; gracious, merciful, slow to anger, of great kindness and repents of the evil. He thinks contrary to us because of our wickedness.

Moreover, the heathen are just like their gods. Are **you** like their god or yours?

7. Brotherly Kindness - The thing about "brotherly" kindness is that a **brother** will be kind when no one else will. A brother (I mean flesh and blood **brother**) will recognize some weakness or flaw in his brother or sister but will choose to love them anyway. Strangers will be kind to someone because that person is nice and deserves the act of kindness. A brother will be kind to his own brother or sister when others have rightly abandoned him or her. (No. I'm not talking about condoning sin.)

Have you ever been "accused" of brotherly kindness?

Is it not amazing that this attribute shows up **after** "Godliness"? It is certainly something that has been sadly lacking in more than one church business meeting! Have you ever been "accused" of brotherly kindness?

8. Charity - Charity is a word with such depth of meaning that modern bible translators are at a loss to define it. Failing miserably to properly explain its depth they simply run to the standard practice of adulterating the word of God and simply changing it to "love". But "love" falls far short of true charity. Webster's 1828 tells us that "charity" entails more than good will or affection for someone. It also includes a desire to **think favorably** toward someone. You can "love" someone that **you know** is a low down rat but you can't honestly "think favorably" about them. To have charity is to possess such a state of mind that you desire to think well of everyone.

Liberal Christians will be quick to swell their chests and claim, “That’s me! I don’t think anything bad about anybody.” But if the previous seven marks of spiritual growth are not evident in them they are only fooling themselves and probably doing more harm than good.

Notice that each list ends with a promise of some great benefit when these traits of mature Christian character permanently reside in our lives. **Romans 5:5** assures us:

5 *And hope maketh not ashamed; because the love of God is shed abroad in our hearts by the Holy Ghost which is given unto us.*

Meanwhile **2 Peter 1:8-11** promises:

8 *For if these things be in you, and abound, they make you that ye shall neither be barren nor unfruitful in the knowledge of our Lord Jesus Christ.*

9 *But he that lacketh these things is blind, and cannot see afar off, and hath forgotten that he was purged from his old sins.*

10 *Wherefore the rather, brethren, give diligence to make your calling and election sure: for if ye do these things, ye shall never fall:*

11 *For so an entrance shall be ministered unto you abundantly into the everlasting kingdom of our Lord and Saviour Jesus Christ.*

Furthermore, you can clearly see how much **pleasure** a child of God would be to his heavenly Father if he could manage to incorporate all of these divine attributes into his own being.

Goin' down deep!

There is yet another gauge of spiritual growth, but rather than being found in a single list it is gleaned from a broad study of Scripture. (That's why we should turn off the TV and bury our noses in the Bible and **study!**)

The Christian life is depicted in three distinct phases of growth. Each segment is progressive and is superior to the one preceding it.

1. Baby - Paul recognized the spiritual immaturity of the Corinthian church and in his first epistle writes in chapter three:

1 Corinthians 3:1, 2

1 *And I, brethren, could not speak unto you as unto spiritual, but as unto carnal, even as unto* ***babes*** *in Christ.*

2 *I have* ***fed you with milk****, and not with meat: for hitherto ye were not able to bear it, neither yet now are ye able.*

The term "carnal" **does not** describe a person living in sin. It describes a person who is not in control of his flesh. Babies do not control their flesh. They don't even try to. They are "carnal." Likewise, a Christian who does not control his flesh is carnal, a babe in Christ.

What do you feed a baby? Milk! The simplest form of nutrition there is. God put everything in milk that a baby needs to grow. Feed a baby a piece of hamburger and it's liable to choke. But it will thrive on milk.

He's a babe. He's carnal. He is not yet in control of his flesh.

The first phase of the Christian life is that of being a **baby**. This early stage is highlighted by the fact that the new convert is **saved** but still not greatly changed from his old life. His hair is still long, he still smokes. His language is such that you'd better not ask him to open a service in prayer and generally there is not a great deal of difference in his outward appearance than that of a lost man. He's a babe. He's **carnal**. He is not yet in control of his flesh. He needs the spiritual **milk** of the word that he might grow thereby. (1 Peter 2:2)

The **milk** of the word of God is the teaching of **basic Bible doctrines**. This baby needs to know what has happened to him. He needs to know about the deity of Christ, the power of His blood, the need to be in church and to be tithing. He needs to hear that Jesus Christ is coming back and that he has fortunately missed the greatest period of tribulation that the world will ever know. He needs to learn to feed himself spiritually through daily Bible reading.

This is light stuff! It is **milk**. He can't handle anything heavier. "Meat" will kill him but milk will sustain him until he can reach the next phase of growth.

2. Teenager - The next great stage in the human life is that of a teenager. Every father remembers the day his son found out there was **steak** out there instead of cereal. The teen years are bold and brash and brazen. Teens are sometimes obnoxious and they love to have it so. They are ready to take on the world. They want to learn all they can and move out toward their next horizon without looking back. They like **meat!**

In Hebrews 5:12-14 we find an excellent picture of someone who is a teenager spiritually:

Hebrews 5:12-14

12 *For when for the time ye ought to be teachers, ye have need that one teach you again which be the first principles of the oracles of God; and are become such as have need of* ***milk****, and not of strong* ***meat****.*

13 *For every one that useth* ***milk*** *is unskilful in the word of righteousness: for he is a* ***babe****.*

14 *But strong* ***meat*** *belongeth to them that are of* ***full age****, even those who by reason of use have their senses exercised to discern both good and evil.*

When a Christian reaches their "teen" years they should be beyond the milk of the word. They should now understand what "Election" is and why John Calvin was so far off.[6] They should now understand that Israel has been set aside by God in this age as He uses the Gentile church to reach the world. He should also know that the setting aside of Israel is by no means permanent. He should understand the Bible dispensationally. He should furthermore be able to engage the critics of the King James Bible in battle and at least hold his own.

These things are **meat**. They take the Christian farther than mere milk. Yet if his pastor can't teach

---

6 In this author's work, *Exploring the Depths of Scripture* is an excellent expose' on what biblical election is and isn't.

these truths his spiritual growth will be retarded. If all he knows is "Soul winning, soul winning, soul winning" he will be ill equipped to face the world in spiritual combat.

But there is a stage of Christian growth that goes even beyond meat. It comes in the later years of a Christian's development.

3. The Man of God - Every **boy** wants to be a man. Every teenager **thinks** he is one. After **milk** comes **meat**. After **meat** comes **grace**. Once again, Paul, in the book of Hebrews explains the mystery as no one else can.

Hebrews 13:9

9 *Be not carried about with divers and strange doctrines. For it is a good thing that the heart be established with* ***grace****; not with* ***meats****, which have not profited them that have been occupied therein.*

"Grace!" We saw it in those five attributes of God in Jonah 4:2. We sadly see its absence all too often in the dealings of Christians one with another. Many, like the spiritual teenagers that they are, beat their chests and attack mercilessly anyone who dares to cross them. They have left the **milk** far behind, they are sustained on a diet of **meat**. But now it is time for **grace**. It is sad that we, the recipients of God's grace, have none in our dealings with each other. We are vicious, vindictive and violent. But worst of all we are so sure that we're "right" that we will destroy anyone who stands in our way.

There is an excellent example of the difference between **meat** and **grace** in the life of the Apostle Paul. In Acts 13 young John Mark departed with Paul and Barnabas on their first missionary journey. But something happened and he returned home. Paul never forgot it. When Barnabas desires to take Mark with them on their second missionary trip Paul balks. He has no intention of letting someone go with them who had already run from the fight. Paul is so adamant that he and Barnabas part company. At this time Paul has been saved approximately 18 years. He's a spiritual teenager, brimming with determination and fight.

But about fourteen years later Paul writes to Timothy that Mark is "profitable to me for the ministry." (2 Timothy 4:11) What has happened? Certainly John Mark has progressed quite a bit since the earlier account. But Paul has passed beyond **meat** to **grace**. He is now willing to overlook Mark's earlier weakness.

What "Grace" Is

As you mature you learn some things. One is that a teenager can get pretty excited about any new truth he has discovered. (Just like **you** did.) You've also been around long enough to realize that you are capable of being **wrong** about something that you were sure you were right about years earlier. Thus, when someone shows more zeal than knowledge, you're willing to give them a little space. You're not going to be quick to judge them. Since there **is** a chance you might be wrong. (Slim. But still a chance.)

Once you grow up a little spiritually you may find yourself more willing to listen to someone of a differing view without seeing the need to destroy them.

Once you grow up a little spiritually you may find yourself more willing to listen to someone of a differing view without seeing the need to destroy them. We all fear anyone with a different view because down inside we fear that they might be right and then we're going to be forced to make a change. It's just easier to kill them!

What "Grace" Isn't

Grace **is not** condoning sin. It is not coming to the defense of someone who has done wrong and who refuses to get right. Sadly, we have an abundance of loose living Christians around today. Suddenly someone gets caught in a secret sin. What do they do? They "repent" of course! But repentance **after** illumination is always suspect. Had Judas repented **before** betraying Christ and turned from his wicked act, his repentance might be more believable.

I once heard of a preacher who got caught in the sin of immorality. He hadn't committed adultery but had done a cheap imitation of former President Clinton. He was caught! What should he do? Well, he knew that if he didn't "repent" his preacher brethren would cut him off. So he did. He even sent a tape out announcing his "repentance." But then on the same tape he all but demanded to be accepted back and continue on in his ministry in a "business as usual" attitude! Should he be forgiven? Yes. Whether or not he has truly repented we cannot know, so we are forced by the Scripture to **assume** sincerity. But should he be trusted? Only by a fool![7]

---

7 Just two short years later it was found that he had been secretly continuing his sin in even greater degradation. He didn't even pretend to repent this time. When his church threw him out he simply went down the road and started a new one with foolish "man followers" who

Moral sins are like going bankrupt. You can have your debt forgiven but don't expect anyone to extend you any credit. The problem with Christianity today is that we not only want forgiveness, we **demand** to be reinstated and pick up right where we left off. No! For some, if they do nothing more than preserve their marriage, God has been merciful to them. You can cry and holler all you want after going bankrupt but no one in his right mind is going to restore their **trust** in you for a long time. Maybe you will never go bankrupt again. But the fact is that nobody knows. Then, after years of paying your bills on time and never welshing on a debt someone may say, "I think he's okay now."

A moral sin pretty well drains a person's bank account of credibility. Will he ever do it again? No one knows for sure. Too often a friend or relative comes riding in on their white horse to demand that the wrongful party be returned to their previous position of trust. They insist that , "We need to have more grace!" They don't really believe that themselves. They're just covering for a friend. If it was an enemy who had done the wrong they would be right there demanding their blood.

---

didn't care what he had ever done.

We need to be careful not to confuse "grace" with stupidity. Voluntarily sticking your head in a hole in the ground and pretending that that is grace will only reek havoc on everyone concerned later.

Growth is a Must

If newborn Christians do not grow they will never be in a position to fulfill Revelation 4:11. They will never be a pleasure to their Creator. It is simply **bigger** than just "Soul winning, soul winning, soul winning!"

CHAPTER FIVE

Holiness vs. Separation

Should we live Separated from the World?

In everything there are extremes. In politics you have the Liberals versus the Conservatives. In lifestyles you have the Hippies versus the Amish. For every position there is an opposite view that goes to the extreme. In Christianity there are those who say we should have no part with the world and those who claim we need to be like them to win them. Which is the correct stand?

The first question that needs answered is: "Does God want us separated from the world?" The answer is relatively simple to locate. In Galatians 1:4 the Apostle Paul tells us that we needed delivered from what he calls "*this present evil world.*" Furthermore, in John 17:11-17 Jesus tells us that we are to be **in** the world but not **of** the world. John himself lets us know in his first epistle that we are not to love the world neither the things in the world. (1 John 2:15-17) Meanwhile

James really lays it on, revealing that "*the friendship of the world is enmity with God.*" Jude says we should even hate the garment that is "*spotted by the flesh.*"

I think we would have to be pretty naive to deny that the world is extremely vile. But we would have to be blatantly dishonest to pretend that God doesn't want His children to separate themselves from the ways and values of "this present evil world." To be honest in this chapter, we need to determine just what "the world" is.

What is "the World"?

The world is not a friend of God nor His people. It is a number of things that are all anti-God. If we can determine what "the world" is we can have some idea of the direction we should be going as representatives of Christ.

1. "The World" is the wrong morals

It doesn't take a genius to figure out that the world and the Bible are at opposite ends of the spectrum when it comes to morals. The world sees nothing wrong with pre-marital sex, adultery or homosexuality. All of which are condemned fiercely in Scripture. Yet the world does not rest with its acceptance of loose living. It promotes it evangelistically in school and college classrooms, books, films and even in the newspapers. Furthermore, the world is so unrelenting in its rebellion against its Creator that it regularly promotes the vilest of men as hero figures. Men like Hugh Hefner, Bob Guzzione, Larry Flynt, Howard Stern and others of their ilk should be driven from the public eye by the righteous railing of the news media. But instead, that very media is a partner in crime with these monuments of immorality.

Films, news magazines and television programs not only show as much nakedness and immorality as they can but they actively promote such acts as "normal," "good" and "healthy." When the most vile man ever to occupy the White House, turned it instead into a whorehouse, the News Mafia was right there not only defending him but murdering anyone who stood against him.

Then if we are to be unlike the world, it is easy to say that we should take note of its moral depravation and **be just the opposite**.

2. "The World" is the wrong music

Music originated as a medium through which man could glorify God. Throughout Scripture we find it being used over and over to exalt and magnify Him. This music was directed at the **spirit** of man. It was designed to help man fulfill Revelation 4:11 in an extraordinary way.

But as the world degenerated music went along with it. Soon we heard about "soul" music. And that's just what it was. Rather than having **God** as its focal point as the music of the spirit, (the classics) it made sinful Man the center of attention. From there, music has been reduced to the sensual. It is now directed at the **body**. It is thundered out without depth in either the tune or lyrics by mangy looking beings, whose language and gyrations while performing, violate every form of decency. The beat is toxic, the words offensive and the performers are repulsive. Both they and their by-product are happily anti-God.

Again, only a diabolical person would try to assimilate such abhorrent clatter into our churches in the name of worship. It has nothing to do with God and is even a proud trademark of the forces of the anti-Christian lifestyle.

So it should be obvious to an honest heart that anyone claiming to love the God of creation should want to separate themselves from this fountain of contamination.

3. "The World" is the wrong education

Worldly education is as aggressive against God as is worldly music. Education is not aimed at equipping a young scholar to glorify God. It is instead designed to harden the young heart against its Creator.

The fantasy of "evolution" is blatantly taught as though scientific evidence upheld it. "Values clarification" is used to drive the last vestiges of morality from the hearts and minds of innocent young victims. The God that made this country great is no longer allowed to be mentioned in the classroom. Christianity is held in disdain by teacher and student alike. Today's educational system is no friend of God...or its student body.[8]

Therefore we should know to be wary of the leavening influences of public education.

We should know to be wary of the leavening influences of public education.

4. "The World" is the wrong goals

The world focuses its praise on vain and inconsequential things. Sports figures are represented as though they were important to life. Someone who can shoot a basket, hit a home run or score a

8 With the turn to total, Godless barbarianism our public schools have added a whole new twist to the term "student **body**."

touchdown is upheld for all to glorify. Talent is exalted higher than the great Creator who bestowed the attribute. To this crowd the least important vocation on earth is preaching, even though a poor, ineffective minister does more good than the greatest basketball player.

So we as Christians should be careful not to incorporate the world's misguided values into our own lives. Sports are a source of minor enjoyment but be careful not to take them too seriously.

Style and fashion are two more worldly distractions that can keep a Christian wasting his energy and resources. Nothing is more shamelessly vain than fashion. And nothing is funnier than watching some vain idiot with a sweater **tied around his neck** because the god of fashion told him that it was the "in" thing to do. Worrying about being in style is far less important than worrying about being **in step** with God.

A Christian who spends his time and money trying to keep up with the latest fashion is guaranteed to waste his time and money on frivolous things of no substantial value. So we, as God's people, should not be putting too much emphasis on keeping in step with fashion.

Another misguided goal of the world is environmentalism. It must be noted that the goal of environmentalism **is not** to "save the earth." Environmentalists are people who have an emotional relationship with dirt. I should imagine a person would have to have failed miserably at every emotional relation in life to feel compelled to turn to the relative safety of dirt. Environmentalists are misdirected in several ways. First, they focus their time and efforts trying to please a non-living entity, the earth. The earth has life **on it** but **it is not alive itself**. But environmentalists feel very righteous as a result of this

The solitary goal of environmentalism is the destruction of the American economy.

love affair with dirt. Of course, loving dirt is a very safe relationship because dirt has never been known to have rejected anyone. In fact, from the seedy look that most environmentalists have, it is probably good that dirt **is** dead and can't reject them or they would fail at that relationship too! Environmentalists have turned their desire to please **away** from God and toward the ground. This is extremely displeasing to the holy God Who made it and them.

But American environmentalism is even worse. The solitary goal of environmentalism is the destruction of the American economy. Most environmentalists are loyal subscribers to the goal of having a one world government. A strong America is the greatest single hindrance there is to that goal. Therefore, it is imperative that America be brought down to the economic level of a third world country. Every objective of environmentalists is to injure the American economy. They couldn't care less about the environment. How do you know? In 1991 Saddam Hussein dumped raw crude oil into the Persian Gulf and set hundreds of oil wells afire. The damage to the Persian Gulf was magnitudes worse than the measly *Exxon Valdez* incident. Yet, just like the arch-liberal N.O.W. organization during Bill Clinton's abuse of Monica Lewinsky, environmentalists were **mute** to this. They should have condemned Hussein as being very near to Adolf Hitler for his vicious attack on their "mother". Yet they were silent. Why? Because they don't care about the environment. They only care about financially shackling the American economy.

So we see that environmentalism is a hateful, dishonest product of the world. Yet many new converts have been deceived into thinking it is a worthy endeavor. No Christ loving Christian should be involved in the pagan rituals of environmentalism.

The World. The perfect "Bad Example"

There is a joke about a man who is such a wretched drunkard that his wife has left him, his children are ashamed of him, he can't hold a job, his health is broken and he is lying in a gutter, homeless. But, instead of being depressed, he enthuses, "My life's not a **total** waste. I can always be used as a bad example!"

The same can be said of the world. It can always be used as a bad example. If a young Christian is uncertain of how they should live their new life they can always look at the world...**and go in the opposite direction**. Yet today many of these very misguided goals are being espoused by our churches. And usually in the name of soul winning. The morality of our culture has been plunged to new depths by public education and the entertainment world. (world?) In order to attempt to draw these casualties of character in, some churches have turned to contemporary "Christian" music. They have heralded environmentalism as a mandatory tenant of the Christian faith. And fashion is alive and well in most Sunday morning style shows.

The new Christian should be hearing messages designed to free their minds of these wayward ideals. They should hear that their solitary purpose for being here is to be a pleasure to their Creator.

Close, but Not Quite

Some groups in Christianity recognize this trend and reject it zealously. They are called "Separationists" ("Legalists" to anyone looking for an excuse not to separate from the world.) Their favorite verse of Scripture is **2 Corinthians 6:17**, *Wherefore come out from among them, and be ye separate, saith the Lord, and touch not the unclean thing; and I will receive you,...* These folks definitely **believe** in separation. They have "convictions" about the length of a man's hair, the length of a woman's hair, the proper dress for each of the sexes, marriage and divorce, where to buy your groceries and just about anything else you can think of and some that you couldn't think of. I have seen where two pages of rules and standards had to be fulfilled before a teenager could attend a church function. Mind you, this is **far better** than the free-for-all that goes on in the modernist churches. But it does get a little overbearing at times.

Are the Separationists wrong? Let's say that they are in the right church but the wrong pew. Basically, most Separationists are militantly determined not to be corrupted by the world. They fully recognize the innate wickedness in the world system and would rather die than have it invade either their families or churches. They are steadfastly turned **away** from the world. Ever looking back to make sure that it does not overtake and thus pollute them. For them the easiest way to curtail the influence of the world is with what has become known as "Checklist Christianity." You can **always** tell when you meet a separationist because they feel compelled to "check you out." It won't take long before they'll be asking you questions like, "Do you go to movies?" "Do you believe in mixed bathing?", "What's your stand on marriage and divorce?" Fail to agree on one point and you'll probably get a sermon on that subject. Failure on two and you shouldn't hold your breath waiting for them to invite you out for fellowship. Miss too many answers and you'll probably be anathematized and be **the subject** of a sermon![9]

---

9 I knew of a preacher who had just taken a church in a small town. Within the first week his church phone rang. The caller very cordially introduced himself; "I'm pastor so-and-so from the other independent Baptist church in town. I just wanted to call you and welcome you to the community. It's a large town and there's room for both of us. I'm looking forward to getting together with you sometime for lunch." Before the startled young pastor could respond his caller continued. "Oh, and I just wanted to ask you some questions to see if we're going to be able to fellowship." (!) He told me later that after about forty-five minutes the man was screaming that he was a heretic and that he would be **preaching against him that Sunday!** (Psalm 133:1)

Behold I show you a Better Way

Separation from the world is good. It is always good. Even if it is for the wrong reason or through the wrong manner. But we are not called to **just** be separated from a corrupt world system. We are called to be **"saints"**! (Romans 1:7, 1 Corinthians 1:2) Saints are **more** than just separated from the world. They are to be **holy**.

When a Christian realizes that they are here with the sole purpose of being a pleasure to the Lord they will examine their life for things that the Lord would find unsavory. We're not to run **from** the world. We are to run **to** the Lord.

When you **love** someone you desire to please them. You find out what they like and do it. You find out what they don't like and don't do it. It's that simple.

If we **love** the Lord we should also want to please Him. We should find what He likes and do it. We happen to know that the Lord wants to be worshiped for the great God that He is. What is the best way to worship Him? Forget your petty opinion and prejudice.[10] God **wrote down what He wants in His Book.**

1 Chronicles 16:29

Give unto the LORD the glory due unto his name: bring an offering, and come before him: worship the LORD in ***the beauty of holiness****.*

Psalm 29:2

Give unto the LORD the glory due unto his name; worship the LORD in ***the beauty of holiness****.*

Psalm 96:9

O worship the LORD in ***the beauty of holiness****: fear before him, all the earth.*

Has a "light" come on yet? Do you have any idea of something you could add to your life that would be a pleasure to your Creator and help you fulfill your obligation of Revelation 4:11? If not, let's see if this will "flip your switch."

1. Our bodies are to be holy - *I beseech you therefore, brethren, by the mercies of God, that ye present your*

10 The one-tracked soul winner will stop here and righteously bellow, "And what could please the Lord more than winning souls?" A little humility on their part might be a good place to start!

bodies a living sacrifice, ***holy****, acceptable unto God, which is your reasonable service.*
(Romans 12:1)

2. The church is to be holy - *That he might present it to himself a glorious church, not having spot, or wrinkle, or any such thing; but that it should be* ***holy*** *and without blemish.* (Eph. 5:27)

3. We are to be holy as individuals - *According as he hath chosen us in him before the foundation of the world, that we should be* ***holy*** *and without blame before him in love:* (Eph. 1:4)

4. Our women are to be holy - *There is difference also between a wife and a virgin. The unmarried woman careth for the things of the Lord, that she may be* ***holy*** *both in body and in spirit: but she that is married careth for the things of the world, how she may please her husband.* (1 Cor. 7:34)

5. The Pastors are to be holy - *But a lover of hospitality, a lover of good men, sober, just,* ***holy****, temperate;* (Titus 1:8)

6. The results of personal holiness -

12 *Put on therefore, as the elect of God,* ***holy*** *and beloved, bowels of mercies, kindness, humbleness of mind, meekness, longsuffering;*

13 *Forbearing one another, and forgiving one another, if any man have a quarrel against any: even as Christ forgave you, so also do ye.*

14 *And above all these things put on charity, which is the bond of perfectness.*

15 *And let the peace of God rule in your hearts, to the which also ye are called in one body; and be ye thankful.* (Col. 3:12-15)

7. He wants us holy at our presentation to Him in Heaven -

21 *And you, that were sometime alienated and enemies in your mind by wicked works, yet now hath he reconciled*

22 *In the body of his flesh through death, to present you* ***holy*** *and unblameable and unreproveable in his sight:* (Col. 1:21, 22)

Now let's look at these areas and see how establishing **holiness** in our lives will not only be a pleasure to God but will take care of the concerns of separation without a list.

1. Our bodies are to be holy - Forget about somebody telling you, "You can't do that." or, "You're not allowed to do that anymore." Instead ask yourself questions such as:

"How can my body be **holy** if I put liqueur in it?"

"How can my body be **holy** if I smoke?"

"How can my body be **holy** if I watch, read or listen to filth?"

"How can my body be **holy** if I............?"

It doesn't take a rocket scientist to see that answering those simple questions will keep you clear of wicked , unclean or just questionable practices as you strive to be **holy** rather than comply with somebody's list.

2. The church is to be holy - The church, the body of Christ, is made up of individual believers. How can **it** be holy if we are not?

The church, local, should not only be **holy** due to the actions of its individual members but should be the prime mover in directing and instructing Christians to be holy.

3. We are to be holy as individuals - Just as there are questions to ask concerning the body there are questions to ask concerning **us**, the soul.

"How can I be **holy** and gossip?"

"How can I be **holy** and try to hurt a fellow Christian?"

"How can I be **holy** and be concerned only with exalting myself?"

"How can I be **holy** and split a church or destroy a preacher?"

"How can I be **holy** and do....**that**?"

These soul searching questions will do far more to prevent havoc in a church than all the sermons on "Touch not God's anointed!" in the world.

4. Our women are to be holy - God made women special. They are wonderful. They are a gift from God. Because they are special to Him, He pays special attention to them in the area of holiness. Their questions may go like this:

"How can I be **holy** in body and in spirit and wear revealing clothing?"

"How can I be **holy** in body and in spirit and dress like a man?"[11]

"How can I be **holy** in body and in spirit and act like a man?"

"How can I be **holy** in body and in spirit and not desire to please the Lord?"

Forget about "legalism". Being **holy** for God will transform the hardest woman into a delicate treasure of God's grace. I've seen it!

---

11 There is **much** debate within Christian circles as to what is proper dress for a woman. I have heard and studied both views. I have a "Litmus Test" which I apply to such questions: If two Christians were arguing their individual positions **and a lost person walked in,** whose side would the lost person take? What side would a lost person take on the "Pants on women" issue? What side would a lost person take on the "New Version" issue? I am loath to take a position that a lost person would join me on. Do you want to?

5. The Pastors are to be holy - Preachers are called of God and as such carry a much greater burden for holiness. He should ask:

"How can I be **holy** and touch a woman in a sensual manner?"

"How can I be **holy** and try to destroy a fellow minister?"

"How can I be **holy** and visit **that** Website?"

"How can I be **holy** and do ungodly things when I'm where no one knows me?"

"How can I be **holy** and be motivated to exalt only myself?"

6. The personal results of holiness - Well what do you know? We **do** have a list! But it isn't a list of "Don'ts". It is rather a list similar to those found in Romans and 2 Peter as gauges of our spiritual growth. Accomplishing holiness in our lives will also result in the additional benefits of: mercies, kindness, humbleness of mind, meekness, a longsuffering attitude, forbearance, a forgiving attitude and, of course, charity.

Look how far into Christian maturity the addition of this one spiritual attribute will take you. Can you imagine what pleasure it must be for the Lord to see these properties blossom in the life of one of His children? There is so much more to the Christian life than just soul winning.

7. He wants us holy at our presentation to Him in Heaven - Notice that the passage eludes to the fact that **we started this life as enemies and aliens**. Yet through salvation in Christ and years of spiritual growth we can be a pleasure to our Creator in a multitude of different ways. But wait! Time and again in the Old Testament we see that a man who had been a **good** king failed the Lord **late in his life**. Imagine having lived a life in a holy manner for years, decades in fact, and then, **one time** an opportunity to be impure comes up that, due to weakness or some other emotional low point, we suddenly find ourselves tempted to surrender to. Think of the years wasted if we indulge.

I **know** you want to be **holy** when you are finally presented to Him in eternity. Don't give in to weakness this late in the game.

In the previous chapter we looked at attributes that need to be added to the Christian life. Let's take a moment to review them, adding the benefits of holiness.

1. Patience
2. Experience
3. Hope
4. Faith
5. Virtue
6. Knowledge

7. Temperance
8. Godliness
9. Brotherly kindness
10. Charity
11. Mercies
12. Kindness
13. Humbleness of mind
14. Meekness
15. A longsuffering attitude
16. Forbearance
17. A forgiving attitude[12]

Isn't it amazing! We end up with a list after all. But it's not a list of things to be removed from your life. It is a list of things to be **added** to your life. And if these attributes are successfully incorporated into your personality over the years you will more than succeed at fulfilling anyone's list of "Don'ts".

The Highest Goal of all

There is great value to separationism. It will, if only by brute force, prevent some Christians from drifting into sin. But, in spite of this separation it will not produce holiness in the individual. That takes years of being submerged in the Bible and walking

---

12 I have consolidated the lists from Romans 5, 2 Peter 1 and Colossians 3, eliminating the duplicates in the process.

circumspectly. And the best part about holiness is that the benefits that **we** receive from it are incidental. For **holiness** in us is **pleasure** to God.

CHAPTER SIX

Desire vs. Convictions

"Love God and do Anything you Want."

It is said that someone accosted C. H. Spurgeon with the charge that Christians weren't allowed to have fun. The above quote was his response. It describes the truth of holiness in one line. If we can love God with all our "heart and soul and mind," there would never be a problem with lists and legalism or liberalism in our churches. Unfortunately, it is not that simple. Therefore the brethren split into two distinct groups at this point. One group wants to use their liberty as an excuse to live just like the world. The other wants us to be different from the world so urgently that they form up lists of "Convictions" that they demand everyone meet. Which is right?

What is a "Liberal"?

The definition is foggy but **the truth** is that most people define a "liberal" as anyone with **one less conviction** than they have. They would never publicly proclaim such a definition but still they behave as though that is their standard. But this is neither accurate nor fair. A liberal is best defined as one who abandons most restraints on their life and pretty much lives to the ease and comfort of his flesh. Most liberals piously hide their weakness to the flesh by demanding "book, chapter & verse" for any objection to their life style. They self-righteously like to claim that if the Bible doesn't specifically forbid something then they are free to indulge in it. (Did you know that there is no "book, chapter & verse" which tells us **directly** not to smoke. Either tobacco or marijuana. This is just a glimpse of how dangerous living your life in the "gray" areas of Scripture can be!) They usually don't **plan** on incorporating fleshy sins into their lives but eventually this is where such unrestrained living ends up. They do not necessarily abandon the foundational doctrines of the Christian faith. They simple take every "liberty" they can when it comes to **un**separated living. Unfortunately many of them become very evangelical in their loose living and tend to be a force for apostasy in churches where their ideals are accepted.

What is a "Legalist"?

Conversely, most Christians label as "legalist" anyone having **one more conviction** than they have. Again, none of them would publicly or even intellectually admit this. Yet this is the criterion by which they judge those with whom they have daily contact.

Now **the fact** is that a true “legalist” is someone who believes that their salvation depends on a measure of **works** rather than the shed blood of the Lord Jesus Christ. But the truth also is that most of those people who are busy labeling everyone they can as a “legalist” do not intend to accuse their adversaries of this. Thus we are left with the original definition.

But actually, those who are labeled “legalist” today are usually well-meaning people who realize there is something wrong with looking and acting like the world. If the Bible refuses to specifically spell out

---

There is something wrong with looking and acting like the world.

---

how a Christian should live, dress or act then they will take it upon themselves to “fill in the blanks” with reams of “standards”, “convictions” and “preferences”. Unfortunately this soon leads to a “holier than thou” contest. Where “legalists” reign supreme there tends to be an overbearing demand to fulfill “the List” and a sad lack of God’s grace with weaker brethren. The “legalist” has his heart in the right place but his methods can be a bit oppressive.

Most legalists like to call the items on their lists, "convictions." That way keeping them becomes imperative for others and proof of their own dedication to Christ. These dreamers define a "conviction" as "something you'd die for." Then list everything from skirt length to where to eat supper. It is highly questionable if they would be willing to die for every item on their list.[13]

How shall we then live?

Some basic values have to be established before the debate can proceed. Should we allow ourselves to be miniature replicas of the world in our life for Christ, or not? I think the Scripture is very clear that God expects us to live differently than does a world that He describes as "evil." Therefore **the spirit** of Scripture favors the "legalist's" **goals** if not his methods. The "liberal" is left ever busy trying to defend and justify a life lived to the pleasure of his flesh.

But intimidation and strong-arm tactics are not the means God uses in Scripture to obtain his will. For certain He is clear to make His desires known but then allows for more grace than we would when it comes to the performance of those directives. More than once

---

13 For the definition of what an actual **biblical** conviction is see this author's work, *Selected Sermons, Vol I.*

we have observed wayward Christians whom God has **not** been quick to judge as we would have been. He very simply **is** what the Bible **says** He is: long suffering. But we should not take unfair advantage of God's kindness as an excuse to let our flesh run our lives. Yet "the List" finds its motivation in **fear**. There are those who are afraid of the reaction of some of their legalistic friends and therefore cow-tow to their friend's list rather than being motivated by a higher ideal. What should be the motivation for truly "separated" living?

The Apostle Paul made one of the most chilling statements in Scripture when he said, *If any man love not the Lord Jesus Christ, let him be Anathema Maranatha.* (1 Cor. 16:22) Here Paul reveals that a Christian can be "saved" and yet live their life under a **curse** if they don't love the Lord. Will they lose their salvation and go to Hell? Of course not. But who wants to live a life where God is their ever present adversary? Who wants God to desire to be a destroyer of their plans rather than One who would give His blessing to them? It is imperative that we **love** the Lord.

Unfortunately everyone knows that you can neither force yourself to love someone nor prevent it. Every man learned this when he was in the sixth grade and fell in "love" with the red haired girl in math class. Even when he knew she hated him he couldn't quench the fire burning in his heart. Nor could he manage to kindle affection for another who, although pretty and kind, he just simply didn't seem to be attracted to. So how can you "force" yourself to love the Lord?

What is "Love"?

Before we define what love **is** we need to explain what it **is not**. Many Christians think that they "love" the Lord because they are **not actively working against him**. This is **not** love. I am presently "not actively working against" the President of the United States but **please** don't mistake that for "love" for him! Love is not **passive**. You didn't "love" every other girl in your sixth grade math class just because you weren't out burning their houses down.

When you **love** someone there are several unavoidable truths present:

1. They are ever in your thoughts.
2. You desire to **always** be with them.
3. You desire for them to be happy.
4. You desire to actively **make** them happy by your actions.
5. You are unable to think ill of them.
6. You refuse to believe anything negative said about them.
7. You want them to see something in you that will make them love you in return.

This is nothing less than prejudice. Moreover it is prejudice **to the maximum degree!** But **this** particular prejudice we call, "love". And it is a wonderful feeling to be overwhelmed by. **Especially** if the object of our affection feels the same way about us as we do about them.

Now look again at the seven particulars that define love. How do they reflect your "love" for the Lord?

1. Is He ever in your thoughts?
2. Do you desire to **always** be with Him?
3. Do you desire for Him to be happy?
4. Do you desire to actively **make** Him happy by your actions?
5. Are you unable to think ill of Him. (Even when He doesn't do what you want Him to?)
6. Do you refuse to believe anything negative anyone says about Him?
7. Do you want Him to see something in you that will make Him love you in return?

Everybody dressed for Somebody, at Sometime in their life

Go back for a moment to the days when you and your spouse were dating. Before you left your house to see them did you not take care that your hair looked good? Did you not wear the nicest clothes you could hoping that they would like them? Did you not do certain things that may have been inconvenient or unusual for you in hopes of pleasing them? **That's not called "legalism", it's called LOVE!** When you love someone you want to dress your best for them. So is it

This motivation of a desire to please someone you love covers every area of our lives.

then wrong to dress your best for the Lord? Not if you love Him. Church isn't a fashion show where each person should seek to "out-dress" the other. It is **God's** place, where each should be concerned with looking their best for Him just as they tried to look their best for their future spouse when they were dating.[14] Why should God be worthy of **less** than you would do for some sinful human?

This motivation of a **desire** to please someone you love covers every area of our lives. When you were dating your wife, weren't you careful of your speech? Then should you not refrain from using some words because they might offend the Lord that you **love**? If we **really** love the Lord would we not voluntarily review our lives and eliminate things that might not please our Saviour. What? You say, "I don't know what could be in my life that is not pleasing to the Lord?" Would you be willing to get down on your knees and **ask** Him in prayer? Would you eliminate anything that He pointed out? Do you **love** Him? But genuine love for the Lord should do more than delete undesirable things from our lives. It should also add some things that are pleasing to the Lord. Don't you believe it would please the Lord to find out you were interested in knowing more about the Book He wrote? Wouldn't it please Him if He saw you turn off your television set and say, "I think I'll just read my Bible tonight."? Wouldn't He be blessed if you dragged

---

14 One of the newest "legalist" doctrines makes the word "dating" equal to "fornication." I became an instant "liberal" for using it. I just fell off someone's list. Considering that I spend most of my time being called a "legalist" I'll accept it for a change.

yourself out of bed Sunday morning and went to church because that was His place and you wanted to be there? Wouldn't if be pleasing to Him to see you eliminate some things from your wardrobe and add others to it because you didn't want to offend Him? Do you **love** Him?

Admit it. You don't Love Him

The sad fact is that most Christians don't really love the Lord. No, they don't **hate** Him, but their lives are not motivated, **changed** by a desire to please Him and Him only, even above themselves. I believe the reason for this is found in Jesus' parable of Luke 7:41-47.

41 *There was a certain creditor which had two debtors: the one owed five hundred pence, and the other fifty.*

42 *And when they had nothing to pay, he frankly forgave them both. Tell me therefore, which of them will love him most?*

43 *Simon answered and said, I suppose that he, to whom he forgave most. And he said unto him, Thou hast rightly judged.*

44 *And he turned to the woman, and said unto Simon, Seest thou this woman? I entered into thine house, thou gavest me no water for my feet: but she hath washed my feet with tears, and wiped them with the hairs of her head.*

45 *Thou gavest me no kiss: but this woman since the time I came in hath not ceased to kiss my feet.*
46 *My head with oil thou didst not anoint: but this woman hath anointed my feet with ointment.*
47 *Wherefore I say unto thee, Her sins, which are many, are forgiven; for she loved much: but to whom little is forgiven, the same loveth little.*

I believe there is a terrible, self-righteous blindness to our own **personal** wickedness. Most Christians, though willing to admit they are sinners, even worthy of Hell, find it difficult to see themselves as truly wicked. As they see it, they are bad, yes, but not **that bad**! They refuse to apply the truth of Jeremiah 17:9 to themselves. Just like the self-righteous lost, they have little trouble finding scores of people who are worse than them. Since they don't see themselves as such really terrible people they don't see the Lord as having had to forgive as much in them as in some others. Therefore, **"the same loveth little."** Since they "love little" they also feel less motivation to change their lives for Christ.

An honest self appraisal

What is needed is twofold. An honest self appraisal and a detailed review of what the Lord has done for you.

1. Jeremiah 17:9 states: *The heart is deceitful above all things, and desperately wicked: who can know it?* That is not a description of Charles Manson or Timothy McVey. It is a description of **you**! Are you willing...are you **able**, to admit that you are as wicked as this verse says you are? Do you **really** accept that your own heart is "deceitful above all things"? (If you don't it shows just how deceitful your heart really is. It obviously has **you** deceived!)

Have you ever done anything that was a little less than sincere? Have you ever done anything that would subtly cause harm to someone you disliked or were angry with? Have you ever tried to promote your own cause but in such a way as to portray yourself as being objective? **That's called deceitful!** That's what your heart is. It's **naturally** that way. You don't even have to work at it.

Have you ever been near death? Almost drown? Trapped in a burning building? Remember the near panic you felt to survive? That's called **desperation**. That is the word God chose to describe the wickedness of your heart. Your heart is desperate to do wickedness. If you have trouble admitting that, it shows just how very wicked your heart is.

You need to view yourself as being as wicked as the Bible says you are. Then maybe you'll agree with God that you are only worthy of Hell. And **then** you might **love** a Saviour Who would go to the cross and take the punishment for **your** wickedness.

2. Furthermore the Bible states in Romans 5:8-9,

8 *But God commendeth his love toward us, in that,* ***while we were yet sinners****, Christ died for us.*

9 *Much more then, being now justified by his blood, we shall be saved from wrath through him.*

There are only two kinds of sin in the world...the sins we brag about, and the sins we're ashamed of. It may be that when you were lost you sat around a table with some of your friends and bragged about some of the wicked things you'd done. But all the time you were bragging you knew things about yourself that you didn't want anyone at that table to find out about. In fact, **even now**, if our friends knew about you what you know about yourself they'd stay away from you. And for you the shame would be unbearable. The fact is that, the only two individuals who **really** know the truth about you are you and Jesus Christ. And He was willing to go to the cross for you, in spite of what He knew about you. (Do you now understand why He may well have looked into the future at your wickedness, while in the garden, and have asked His Father to "let this cup pass from me."?

Maybe He thought you were just too undeserving of salvation!)

If your parents, your spouse, your children or your friends knew about your secret sins they would break fellowship with you. Some would go on a violent campaign against you. **And you would deserve it!** In fact, there have probably been times when you have not been able to even love yourself because of what you knew about yourself. Yet when Jesus Christ knew these things **He loved you when you couldn't love yourself**. No one has **ever** loved you like that.

Now, have you been forgiven **much** or little? Then how should you love the Lord?

More than a Saviour

One of the major mistakes people make after their salvation is to view Jesus Christ as nothing more than their Saviour. They are "saved" from a Hell they've never experienced to a Heaven they can't comprehend. This sometimes makes it easy to place little value on what the Lord has done for them. Someone once said, "We place little value on that which has cost us little and great value on that which has cost us greatly." Since our salvation has cost us **nothing** personally, we can have a tendency to place little value on it. Since the Lord has bestowed on us something that we're really not going to use until we die, it seems to demand no great debt from us here. This attitude is wrong and must be overcome.

If the Lord had left you in the ditch where He found you when He saved you, you'd still be better for the experience.

I have often said while preaching, "If the Lord had **left** you in the ditch where He found you when He saved you, you'd still be **better** for the experience... But I don't know anybody He did that with." Many come to the Lord at a time of crisis. It may be legal, financial, marital, mental or some other of the many problems that plague us on our journey through time. The Lord saves them. If He did no more than that they would still benefit eternally from that experience. But in every case I've seen the truth of 2 Corinthians 5:17 immediately comes into play, *Therefore if any man be in Christ, he is a new creature: **old things are passed away**; behold, **all things are become new**.*

Our churches are full of people who would be divorced if it were not for the Lord. Some would be in prison. Some would be in mental health facilities. Their salvation was **more** than just a "fire escape" from Hell. It was a new life.

It is possible that your heart has not kindled a proper love for the Lord because you have not considered the total value of all the things He did for you **besides** salvation. Let's examine some of His miracles and see if any compare to your personal situation.

1. Salvation - We must start with salvation. Your salvation is more than a free trip to Heaven. It is a commodity that cost God a very great deal, the life of His only begotten Son. The immense truth of 2 Corinthians 5:21 needs to be comprehended, *For he hath made him to be sin for us, who knew no sin; that we might be made the righteousness of God in him.* Jesus Christ was the only perfect man ever to live. He was completely righteous. He is the only man that ever lived who **deserved** eternity in Heaven. But He did more than die for our sins. He **became sin** for us so that we could **become righteousness** through Him. That righteousness was just as undeserved on our part as the degradation was on His. Again, **no one** has ever loved you like that. He deserves our love.

2. Sanity - I have talked to more than one Christian who had serious mental problems prior to their redemption. Some had been taking personality altering drugs. Some had experienced shock therapy. Some had spent time in mental institutions yet following their conversion the Lord restored their minds. Are you one of those? Can you not find a deep seated love for what He has rescued you from?

3. Marriage - Countless couples have come to the Lord due to counseling they were receiving to attempt to save a shipwrecked marriage. Marriage counseling had failed. The advice of friends and loved ones had not turned their situation around. All seemed hopeless. Yet some of those very people are reading this book right now, happily married to the spouse they once thought they were destined to lose. Have you thanked God for His mercy?

On the other hand there are others who were unmarried when they came to Christ. But due to the life they lived prior to salvation they did not merit a happy marital relationship. Yet the Lord saw fit to allow their life to intercept that of another precious Christian and today they experience a marital bliss that they realize everyday they do not deserve. How could you not love such a gracious God?

4. Money - Many who now claim the name of Christ were sluggards and slackers. Life prior to Christ was a daily routine of finding a way to make a living without working. Or, in some cases, it was nothing more than a series of well intended but unwise ventures that resulted in failure. Then the Lord redeemed them and graciously set them in a place where they now enjoy a comfortable, secure living. Have you thanked God for each of His blessings?

5. Friendship - Some folks were without a friend when they came to Christ. For some it was their own fault. Demanding, crude, unsociable, they completely changed following their adoption by God and have allowed the Bible to alter their personality to the point that they now enjoy the fellowship of scores of friends.

6. Family - Many people hale from families that are somewhat less than perfect. They were unloved and unwanted. Their minds retain no precious family memories. No one anticipates a call from them. Yet, after coming to Christ, God graciously allowed them to become part of a family that laughs and loves and functions far better than any psychologist would want to admit. Should you not kneel right now and thank God for what He has done for you **beyond** your salvation?

7. A future - Many were destined to end up in jail or a menial job or standing under a bridge holding a sign that says "Will work for food." Tomorrow, to them, meant one more worthless day just like today. Then God took them and made them a church member or a deacon or a Sunday School teacher or a Preacher. Now each day holds a new wonder of the magnificence of their gracious Saviour. Do you now have a future that you never dreamed could be yours?

Add it All Up

I am sure that I have barely scratched the surface when it comes to the multitude of blessings that **accompany** salvation. You should sit down with a pen and paper and take inventory of the countless blessings, large and small, that our gracious Creator has showered on you since your surrender to Him. Perhaps that is what it will take to awaken your heart and have it begin to generate the love that He is worthy of. Perhaps then you won't need a "list" to force you to conform to someone's perception of godliness. Perhaps then you will thankfully and willingly eliminate some things from your life that don't lend themselves to holiness and introduce some things into your life that, though foreign to you, are becoming to a Christian. "Desire" will trample a "list" to death in an effort to please a benevolent Saviour.

CHAPTER SEVEN

Bible Knowledge vs. Bible Ignorance

The Bible is the only thing that you can hold in your hand that God has given you. It is also His sole source of communication with man. I would say, therefore, that that would qualify it as being uniquely important in our efforts to get to know our Creator.

Someone once said, "Power corrupts. Absolute power corrupts absolutely." This statement shows great insight into the wayward heart of man and the intoxicating effect that too much authority has on him. Yet amazingly, this rule is not an absolute truth. Why? Because **no one** has absolute power like our Creator does and yet He is in no way corrupt. Think for a moment. If you have absolute power you can be as mean as you wish to be. After all, if you have absolute power, **who can stop you?** Yet, in spite of His immense power, He is benevolent rather than vicious.

He is kind rather than cruel. He is righteous rather than wicked. He is loving rather than mean. When you ponder the fact that He can do **anything** to you at **anytime** and yet He would prefer to bless you, it is astonishing. Why would any of His creatures not desire to know more about Him? Why would any of His creatures not desire a closer relationship with Him? Yet, how do you go about that? Throw a virgin in a volcano?

Fortunately God has even made this quest relatively simple. He wrote us a **Book**. This holy volume is the only source of input we have from Him. Some would tell us that He glows regularly in their bedrooms giving them decrees on how to raise money. Others would try to persuade us that He stands 950 feet tall in their backyard telling them how to raise money. Some would liken Him to a gangster who would threaten one's life for not raising enough money. It seems that the God people reveal **outside of Scripture** is interested in nothing more than making a chosen few filthy rich! But if you are deceived, it is your own fault. God revealed Himself to all of us equally through Scripture. If you read His Book you would get to know the author better.

Reading a book is more than a shallow endeavor. When you read a book, you read the author. Some years ago I had a meeting in a church where I had never been before. On my first night there a man approached whom I had never met nor spoken with. He said, "I've read your *Answer Book* three times. From reading it three times I feel like I already know you." How could that happen? Simple. When you write a book you do more than convey information. Whether you want to or not you permeate the text with your personality. In addition to the facts this man had read in my book, he had further experienced my personality. Therefore, he felt a relationship with someone he had never met.

God wrote a Book. It is filled to overflowing with history, science, humor, morality and simple stories. Yet far beyond that, He has infused its text

Without reading the Bible God will never be anything more than an opinion you hold about Him.

with His personality. He has left an invisible imprint across its text from cover to cover. Invisible? Yes. You can get a concordance or a Bible program to chase down any word that interests you in the Bible. You can scan its pages for any particular story or fact that interests you. But in doing so the personality of God will be invisible to you. It cannot be seen in a computer printout. It cannot be captured by an arbitrary list of verses. You may even be able to define God as you wish and find “book, chapter & verse” to prove your thesis and still have the God of Scripture remain a total stranger to you. Without reading the Bible God will never be anything more than an opinion you hold about Him. If you don’t read the Bible personally then all you will ever know about God will be what someone else tells you. This does not have to be. He gave you the Book and gave you a reasonable amount of intelligence. Now use them to get to know the God Who holds the power you use to draw each breath.

Amos said it, That Settle's It

The prophet Amos warned us that a famine was coming our way. In Amos 8:11 he said, *Behold, the days come, saith the Lord GOD, that I will send a famine in the land, not a famine of bread, nor a thirst for water,* ***but of hearing the words of the LORD:*** Some have interpreted this to mean that the day will come that you can no longer obtain a Bible. That will never happen. For all of its flaws, the computer age has assured us that the Bible will **never** become unobtainable. When the Communist Chinese were ruthlessly trying to subdue the spirit of freedom in China a few years ago, they found that they no longer could control the information streaming from the world’s largest concentration camp. Freedom fighting students simply faxed or e-mailed information out of the country and the system was too broad for the heartless Communist dictators to thwart.

If some grand power could knock on every door in our nation (it's **bigger** than you can imagine) and confiscate every copy of Scripture available, some folks would be generating a new copy from the Internet before the Gestapo finished with their street. And it would be **King James** Bibles at that!

Amos didn't say there would be a famine of the word of the LORD itself. He said there would be a famine of **hearing** the words of the LORD. This day has arrived. I recently read a book by a raving madman who declared that **every message** preached in our churches should be an **evangelistic** message. Not that the Gospel should be mentioned. Rather it must be at the heart of every sermon preached. This from a fool who would have us believe he preaches the "whole counsel" of God. I saw another book recently that listed hindrances to soul winning. It could be summed up with one sentence. "Bible teaching of any kind other than the plan of salvation."

This kind of rabbling comes from men who **are not** students of Scripture. The only thing worse than being biblically ignorant is being biblically ignorant around others who **are not**. It's embarrassing. It also prevents some would-be dictator from conning people into obeying him. Bible knowledge is a threat to the preacher too lazy or too dishonest to read the Book himself. It will hinder his every attempt to "pull rank" on his listeners.

Books are Not Decorations

We have all gone into a restaurant and seen a shelf full of beautifully bound books used as part of the decor of that facility. No one in the place knows what's **in** those books and no one cares. Some preachers actually purchase books valued only on how they will look on their library shelf. I am an author. I have written about a dozen books. I never penned **one** hoping that it would do no more than decorate the library shelf of some deadhead preacher while he whiled away his time playing computer games! One of the greatest compliments you can pay an author is to tell them, "I read your book."

God is an author. He has written a Book. It is different than any other work ever penned. It is the **only** Book on earth that is Divinely inspired. It is the only one He wrote. Are you so foolish as to think that He wrote it because it would make a nice addition to your library shelf? If God wrote a Book that He never intended people to read it was the greatest waste of Divine effort in all of time! While some gods have provided their feeble followers a few meaningless rituals, ours has provided us a Book. While some gods have limited knowledge about themselves to an exclusive class within some religious sect, our God has made His personality available to anyone who cares to read His Book. One thing God has **never** done is acted in vain. Yet, if He inspired the Bible without intending it to be read, then all of His efforts were in vain. We are **duty bound** to read this message from our Creator. How can we hope to deceive Him into thinking we are interested in Him, that we "love" Him, if we have no interest in the Book He wrote?

Read the Book!

Everywhere I go I promote Bible reading. It's one of few truly **self-serving** things a preacher should do. I have often pointed to my book table and declared, "Don't buy my books! Don't read a **book** about a **Book** that you don't read." It is insanity to collect and read books **about** the Bible and not read the Book that those books are about!

The most efficient Bible reading program I've found consists of reading a Proverb for the day's date. That puts you through the Book of Proverbs once a month. But more importantly, that puts the Book of Proverbs **through you** once a month. In addition to this, there is no valid excuse why every Christian can't read a minimum of **ten pages** of the Bible **everyday**. Before you go ballistic and start whining about that being too much stop and think for a moment. (That's about all most television oriented Christians can manage.) How much time do you spend watching television? Did God **inspire** your television program. (Forget the "Christian" broadcasting junk!) Do you read other books? No matter what book it is it **isn't** inspired. The **only** inspired words in this book are where I quote the Bible. So you've sat down with an **uninspired** book and read 50 or 60 or 70 pages at a sitting. Now how are you going to explain to God that you thought nothing of reading 100 pages of Louis La'Mour or Tom Clancy or Janette Oke and yet thought that a mere **ten** pages of **His** Book was an unreasonable amount? (I'm glad I'll be there to hear your feeble excuse. It should be good for a thousand-year laugh.)

Jesus Christ quoted Deuteronomy 8:3 when He stated, *But he answered and said, It is written, Man shall not live by bread alone, **but by every word that proceedeth out of the mouth of God**.* in Matthew 4:4. Note that Jesus didn't just specify Psalm 23. He didn't recommend solely the Sermon on the Mount. Now **how** are you going to "live" by **every** word of God if you don't **read** every word of God? You should start at page 1 and read ten pages a day until you've finished your Bible. **Then you should do it again**. Then do it again. And keep doing it until you **die** or until you hear a **real loud trumpet**!

Do you really know God?

Most lost people don't really know God. They simply frame a mental picture of Him that basically sees anything they do as "not being all that bad." Unfortunately, most Christians' view of God differs little from this. They and "the god of their mind" are always in agreement. He is very pleased that they aren't as others. He has sworn to provide them with "life, liberty and the pursuit of happiness." This is what is known as "creating God in our own image." You think, "He may be upset with others but not with me. He really appreciates the way I am." This view is so shallow and self-serving as to be an insult to a holy God. Did you know that **God** is different than you? Did you know that **His** goals are far more important than yours are? Did you know that He is **never** wrong? What? You say you believe that? Then you acknowledge that He was **not** in error when He allowed the **innocent** servants of Job to be killed in Job chapter one. He was absolutely correct when He took the life of Ezekiel's wife in Ezekiel 24:16-18. He was not incorrect to force Hosea to marry a harlot. He wasn't wrong to have Isaiah walk around naked for three years! (Isa. 20:2) You say, "Well, I don't think Isaiah was actually **naked**." You'd better read verse 4! You further believe He was not unreasonable when He had a man stoned to death just for picking up sticks on the Sabbath. (Num. 15:32-35) Wait a minute! Do some of these actions upset you? Do some of the actions of **your God** seem unreasonable and even cruel? Didn't you say God is **never** wrong? So if He does something that doesn't sit well with you, something that you'd be

God was absolutely correct when He took the life of Ezekiel's wife.

tempted to see as "wrong",then doesn't that tell you that **you are the one that's wrong**? It is no failing on the part of God. It is a failing on **your part** for not being so like Him that you can't readily agree with His righteous actions![15] If you read His Book you might get to know Him well enough to quit being ever sympathetic to **Man** and start cheering for **God**. He's not "wrong," He's **righteous**. And that righteousness is so foreign to you that you find it offensive. And **nothing** will change your misguided thinking but exposure to the Book that your God wrote.

---

15 Admit it. Not only did some of these actions upset you, but this was the first time you even knew they had taken place. **That's** how ignorant you are of your God and His Book.

Before you write this God up as cruel you had better remember that this is the same God that provided His only begotten Son so that He could suffer to make the payment for your sins. A payment that you couldn't afford to make yourself. This is the same God that saved you when you called on Him. This is the same God that has been so very gracious to you over the years. And he wasn't wrong then either!

The Bible is deeper than the page

A God that can **speak** the universe into existence in six days is no shallow individual. Anyone Who can design the interlocking systems in nature has some depth to Him. The designer of the human eye is definitely a thinker. His depth of character has been imparted to the Scripture. The Bible is much deeper than the mere words on the page. There is far more to the Word of God than the plan of salvation. Why would someone who claims to be God's son not be interested in reading and studying his Father's book?

Most "Bible" colleges are staffed by men who spend little to no time investigating Scripture. Those few who give Bible study any time have usually been sidetracked by "the nuggets from the Greek" to the point of nausea. How many of you have heard some "humbly-proud" professor boast that, "I do all my personal devotions from the Greek." To which I am impelled to exclaim, "Why!?" The answer is, **Pride!**

That's why they do their personal devotions from "the Greek." They're looking to find something they can impart to a weaker Christian. They believe that **all** Christians are "weaker" than they are because they can't read "the Greek." They love the heady feeling of intellectual superiority that being able to spout a few Greek words provides. The most dangerous person in their congregation is the one who desires to learn more about the Bible.

One of the first things a young Christian should interest themselves in is basic Bible doctrine. Salvation by grace, the eternal security of the believer, the need for water baptism following salvation, the importance

---

If he can teach the Bible without making an error then he's God!

---

of the local church, proofs of Christ's deity, His resurrection and His soon return. Most Bible colleges do a fair job at conveying these to the young believer. But a realization has to take place in the students mind.

I remember being in Bible college shortly after being saved. I came to a strange conclusion about my teacher. (This is equally true of **all** Bible teachers.

Including me.) If he can teach the Bible **without making an error** then he's God! Since I knew he wasn't God I figured that he had to be wrong somewhere even if I didn't know where. I didn't immediately seek to locate something in his teaching that I could consider an error. I simply kept this truth in mind so I wouldn't be too taken by man. When this conclusion is reached it is easy to say to yourself, "I'll just find out where he's wrong, correct it and then...**I'll be God!** Nope. Forget it. No one can escape their own fallibility.

But this is not an excuse to stop seeking the truths buried in Scripture. If God put something in the Bible "in between the lines" we pay Him a great compliment by seeking to enlighten ourselves by finding it. Yet some can't even recognize the difference between the Old and New Testaments. And they will crucify anyone who delves into Scripture for the truth. That is not to say that we need to be bent on uncovering some deep, dark new doctrine and then proclaim it to any and all we meet. It means that we shouldn't be ignorant of our Father's Book. Would it not be great flattery to God if He saw us spending more time seeking new things in His Book than we spend watching television? More time than we spend learning the career facts about some insignificant football player?

Whadayaknow, Joe?

There should be some desire to better know the Bible that should spark your interest enough to cause you to put down your remote and open your Bible and study:

1. Did Jonah **die** when he was in the whale's belly?

2. Where in the Bible does the term, "Godly line of Seth" appear?

3. Where in the Bible does the term, "Looking forward to the cross" appear?

4. What will come **after** the Millennium?

5. Who holds the "Title Deed" to the earth?

6. Is the mid-Tribulation rapture of Matthew 24:27-31 **our** rapture or someone else's?

7. What nut made it into the Holy of Holies?

8. What is the "holy thing" mentioned in Lev. 27:22, 23 and Who fulfills that position in the New Testament?

9. What are the five crowns available to the Christian as rewards at the Judgement Seat of Christ?

10. Which angel is God's "Warrior" and which is His "Spokesman"?

Now immediately some shallow, biblically ignorant soul winner, who has no idea of what he just read, will spout, "Well bless God. What difference does it make when souls are going to Hell?!" But that is a naked admission of being **comfortable** in their biblical ignorance. Stop and think! (I know it's difficult without Dan Rather to direct you.) Did God write the Bible? Yes. Well, if He put something in the Bible, is it important? Yes. What if He veiled some of those things to see how serious we were about learning His Book? Should we expend the time and effort to investigate this Book? Well?

Do you not think that our Creator would be **blessed** to see us spending time trying to unfold the mysteries He has implanted in His message to us? If He put "deeper things" in the Bible with no intention of us finding them then He was wasting His time. Will we not be better Christians if we expose ourselves to more and more of the truths of Scripture. **Will too much Bible hurt you?** Are you "sports smart" but "biblically stupid"? Are you "computer literate" but "biblically retarded"? Are you interested in the things of this world enough to spend time studying them but couldn't care less about what God has for you. Just how do you intend to convince Him that He means something to you?

Don't be Intimidated!

Intimidation is a coward's cheap method of controlling those around him. When facts or affection are missing, bluff and bluster will usually work to bully a lesser person into acquiescing to their will. If you are so lacking in character that you bend your knee to someone who "leans" on you then you need to repudiate Jesus Christ and get down and worship your **real** god, your authoritarian dictator. What is it about Bible knowledge that some preacher's fear? Why would a pastor wish to keep His people biblically ignorant? It is most likely one of several possibilities:

1. Laziness - Some preachers have no personal reason for keeping their people from investigating the Bible. They, themselves, are simply too busy with things of lesser, **much lesser,** importance and have no intention of "wasting" their "valuable" time spending hours pouring over Scripture. It is imperative that this person squelch any interest in Bible study among his people or they may start wondering why **he** isn't doing it.

2. Convenience - Many preachers haven't learned anything new from Scripture since the day they graduated from Bible college. Now they are busy with "The Alumni Association" and sporting an honorary doctorate from their "Alma Mater". They realize that if they begin to study their Bible and fail to walk in lock-step with their alumni brethren they may face some intimidation and rejection of their own. After years of putting all of their eggs in one basket they cannot afford a little Bible truth to come between them and success.

3. Exposure - There are a very few men in the ministry who are down right crooks. They are not sincere. They are not in love with Christ. They couldn't care less about their people. They have simply found that preaching beats working. These professionals are interested in nothing but power and income. They bully anyone who dares to threaten their scam. These "Lord's Anointed" will absolutely destroy anyone who gets in their way. The Bible holds no interest to them and, in fact, threatens their security, just like it did for Jimmy Jones.

4. Too much to lose - Some preachers have some hidden sins in their lives. Outwardly they appear clean. Yet secretly they are living a double life. These men know that if they study their Bible they will be forced to change for one of two reasons:

A. They will be faced with plain Scripture that condemns their actions.

B. The spiritual input from that Book will lead to conviction and they will experience no peace until they submit to God's dealing.

It is far easier to maintain a spirit of biblical ignorance!

5. Misguided - Some preachers simply know no more than what they were taught in Bible college. They have no idea that **anything** could compare or outshine soul wining in importance. They have no idea that the Bible contains anything more than the plan of salvation and a few inspirational sermon texts. They are ignorant. But they are innocent. They have never risen higher than their teachers and never suspected that it was possible.

Many Christians are intimidated by a preacher who holds a tight reign on them.[16] It may be their pastor. It may be the man who led them to Christ. It may be some great preacher. It is not wrong to love or admire a person who has done much for you and perhaps spared you great grief. But **remember!** You owe no debt to be biblically ignorant to **anyone**.

Up or down, the Choice is Yours

Throughout history there have been some great spiritual awakenings. It was the Great Awakening of the 1700's that led directly to the establishment of the United States. This awakening happened when God's people returned to Scripture.

---

16 No matter how sincere **you** might be, don't use the Bible nor anything I've written as an excuse to cause your pastor grief. Don't be confrontational with him. Don't work behind his back to pressure him. If you do you are a spiritual criminal. You are **not** godly. **Don't you ever hurt a church!**

There have also been many great denominational movements. Martin Luther sparked the Reformation when he turned to Scripture for authority rather than a man. The Congregationalists, Methodists and Presbyterians, not to mention the Southern Baptists were once great forces for righteousness. This was due to the great importance they put on Bible knowledge at that time. Yet, as the years have gone by, these great denominations have wandered from Scripture and placed their emphasis in less important areas. America is sprinkled with closed old Congregational and Methodist campgrounds. Many old white clapboard churches stand empty because their ministers, and then their congregations abandoned the Book that made them great. Presently we are seeing the Southern Baptists slide ever farther from Scripture. These once mighty denominations are having to consolidate congregations, welcome worldliness and even ordain women in a vain attempt to survive.

I travel the entire United States in one giant circuit that takes three years to complete. I preach in **King James, Bible believing, Baptist** churches. These churches are **constantly growing**. They are buying, building or adding on to their present facilities. This is not all based on the "Soul winning, soul winning, soul winning!" philosophy that spawned the hollow church growth of the '70's. These churches are pastored by men of diverse and contrasting personalities. But they have one thing in common. They promote, "Bible, Bible, Bible" to their people. They have no fear of a congregation that is immersed in Scripture. They are eager to "edify the saints" with every Bible truth they can, **as well as** soul winning.

It is **the Bible** that makes us different from the world. It is also **the Bible** that makes us different from the rotting corpses of the once mighty denominations. If we abandon this divine Book in favor of anything, no matter how noble sounding, we will soon see our churches promote "Huggy Christianity" with worldly music to entertain carnal congregations as we become more and more like "this present evil world." Only being "Bible People" can prevent that.

CHAPTER EIGHT

His "Ultimate" Pleasure

Unfortunately, due to Hollywood and the constant stream of filth that pours from it, the words "pleasure" and "ultimate pleasure" have taken on a singular meaning that they shouldn't have. Americans have sunk to the depths where they can watch some mouth-breathing idiot pop the top on a can of beer and exclaim, "Fellers, It don't git no better'n this!" and believe it is true. They have lowered themselves to the place where they can't talk about "pleasure" without acquiring a sly, knowing smile and a wink. But regardless of the cesspool mentality that has been infused into the minds of all Americans by their television god, lost and saved alike, we are **still here for God's pleasure**. And that has **nothing** to do with Hugh Hefner's job or Howard Stern's vocabulary!

When a person gets saved they have finally arrived at a place in their existence where they can fulfill Revelation 4:11 and be a pleasure to their

Creator. That moment, when their spiritual birth takes place, **is not** an ending. It is a beginning. At that moment they begin a new journey in their life where they will have opportunity after opportunity to make changes and adjustments in their life to increase the

If God can't tell you what to get out of your life then forget it.

pleasure they are to their Creator. They should start each day asking God, "What can I do to put a smile on **your** face?", rather than telling Him how **He** can put a smile on **their** face. They need to shut all outside interference out and ask **Him** if He approves of their music, their dress, their friends and their lifestyle. They don't need anyone's "list" and they don't need to be poisoned by some carnal Christian who spends all their time justifying their worldly ways with the word, "liberty, liberty, liberty." If God can't tell you what to get out of your life then forget it. But woe be unto you if you harden your heart when He speaks.

Just as surely as there are things in a new Christian's life that need to be deleted, there are things that are lacking in the life of a lost man that need to be added to the life of a Christian. The need to learn the Bible mandates regular church attendance. Bible reading is as important spiritually as our daily meals are physically. Tithing comes not too far behind. One by one God will begin to show His new child what is expected of him. And each change is to the benefit of both God and man. (In that order.) This isn't a one way street.

The Christian life is one of daily minor and a few major conflicts that all give us an opportunity to be the pleasure to our Creator that we were meant to be. The successful Christian is the one who manages to put a smile on the face of their Creator **everyday**. And that takes a lot more than mere soul winning. Our sacrifices, decisions and zeal should be a regular source of delight to our Creator. Yet there may be a source of **ultimate** pleasure for Him which may just define the very essence of our existence.

The Test

The Bible makes it clear that God never tempts a man to **sin**. (James 1:13, 14) Yet it also makes it surprisingly clear that He regularly **tests** His people:
1. Psalm 11:4 *The LORD is in his holy temple, the LORD's throne is in heaven: his eyes behold,* ***his eyelids try, the children of men***.

2. Jeremiah 6:27 *I have set thee for a tower and a fortress among my people, that thou mayest know and* ***try their way***.

3. Jeremiah 9:7 *Therefore thus saith the LORD of hosts, Behold, I will melt them,* ***and try them****;*
for how shall I do for the daughter of my people?

4. Jeremiah 17:10 *I the LORD search the heart,* ***I try the reins****, even to give every man according to his ways, and according to the fruit of his doings.*

5. Daniel 11:35 *And some of them of understanding shall fall,* ***to try them****, and to purge, and to make them white, even to the time of the end: because it is yet for a time appointed.*

6. Zechariah 13:9 *And I will bring the third part through the fire, and will refine them as silver is refined,* ***and will try them as gold is tried****: they shall call on my name, and I will hear them: I will say, It is my people: and they shall say, The LORD is my God.*

7. Revelation 3:10 *Because thou hast kept the word of my patience, I also will keep thee from the hour of temptation, which shall come upon all the world,* ***to try them that dwell upon the earth***.

In fact, the Bible records that we are to desire this testing:
1. Psalm 26:2 *Examine me, O LORD, and prove me; **try my reins and my heart**.*

2. Psalm 139:23 *Search me, O God, and know my heart: **try me**, and know my thoughts:*

God can't force us to love Him. That wouldn't be real love.

Now examine again the reason for our existence: the sole pleasure of our Creator. If the minute sacrifices of the daily Christian life are a **standard**, continual pleasure to our God, then what would be the **ultimate** pleasure we could provide Him?

Every Bible believer knows that Man's heart is basically turned away from God naturally. We also know that God, our Creator loves us and desires for us to love Him in return. Now, how can God find out if we **really** love Him? He can't **force us** to love Him. That wouldn't be real love. He would need a way to test our love to see if we put His interests ahead of ours. What could be our **ultimate** act of love for Him so that our love for Him would be undoubtable? Surely you **do** understand that there is more to loving the Lord than merely **saying** you do? How can you prove that love?

I have often pointed out that the only way you can prove your love for someone is by how much you're willing to **sacrifice** for them. Every slimy, filthy man who has ever beguiled an innocent young lady with the words, "If you love me, you will." understands that. When we sacrifice our **time** to be with someone it shows our affection for them. When we sacrifice our **money** to buy them something it further establishes the proof of our love. Then, when we **give up a life lived alone** to marry another we have proven the depth of our love. We put **sacrifice** above **self** to prove our love.

When Jesus Christ went to the cross His sacrifice was the **ultimate** proof of God's love for us. (Romans 5:8, 9.) Even if you reject Christ and go to Hell you cannot honestly question the sincerity of God's love for you. We could never equal God's sacrifice in proving our love to Him.

But the real test of our love is if we make our sacrifice voluntarily. Without coaching or pressure from the recipient. Therefore, if we are going to ever **really prove** our love for God we are going to have to come to something in our lives that will **test** our sincerity. Where we will have the opportunity to choose between Him and us. Passing this test would be the **ultimate** pleasure we could be to our Creator, for then He would **know** that we loved Him above ourselves. Peter calls this our "fiery trial."

This test has only one question; "Whom do you love more? You or Me?"

Examples, Please!

It would only seem fit that God would undoubtedly test **every** one of His children to try their "love" for Him. But He obviously wouldn't record **every** test of every Bible character in His Book. Yet I believe we do have several examples. Two, in fact, are tests without a doubt for the text of Scripture identifies them as such.

1. Abraham - God makes it very plain in Genesis 22:1 that what ensues is nothing more than a **test** of Abraham's love for Him: **Genesis 22:1** *And it came to pass after these things, that* ***God did tempt Abraham****, and said unto him, Abraham: and he said, Behold, here I am.*

The Test: Will Abraham put God or himself first?

Answer: God
Score: 100%
The Result: God was well pleased.

2. Hezekiah - In 2 Chronicles it states that the visit by the Babylonian officials was a test:
2 Chronicles 32:31 *Howbeit in the business of the ambassadors of the princes of Babylon, who sent unto him to inquire of the wonder that was done in the land, God left him,* ***to try him****, that he might know all that was in his heart.*

The Test: Will Hezekiah put God or himself first?

Answer: Self

Score: 0

The Result: His grandchildren ended up captives. (2 Kings 20:17, 18.)

It seems that something from as innocent as; showing off your greatness and not giving God credit for it, to being willing to sacrifice a son, can be the parameters for the test. It also seems that the results are devastating if we fail our test. In Hezekiah's case people died and his descendants ended up in captivity.

With these parameters in mind, let's see if we can identify what may have been the ultimate test of some other Bible characters.

3. Adam - It is obvious that God wanted to see if Adam would choose himself over God. He had made man. Now He needed to find out if man would love Him first.

The Test: Will Adam put God or himself first?

Answer: Self

Score: 0

The Result: The whole world is cursed. Death reigns over man.

4. Jacob - I believe Jacob's test came at Penuel when he wrestled with the angel. It had to do with him facing his brother Esau. Somehow he passed. It may be that he went out **before** Leah and her children to die if he must rather, than hide behind a wife he didn't love.

The Test: Will Jacob put God or himself first?

Answer: God

Score: 100%

The Result: No one dies although there was clearly the potential for it.

5. Moses - Moses was a great man in the eyes of Israel. When they asked for water God told Moses to **speak** to the rock. Instead he smote it. God was not exalted by this. (Num. 20:12)

The Test: Will Moses put God or himself first?

Answer: Self

Score: 0

The Result: He and Aaron die short of seeing the Promised Land.

6. David - David's test had nothing to do with Bathsheba. That was a problem he had with his **flesh**.

But in 1 Chronicles 21:1 he obeys the devil (as Adam did) and chooses to number Israel. (Pride!)

The Test: Will David put God or himself first?

Answer: Self

Score: 0

The Result: 70,000 people die in a three day pestilence.

7. Nehemiah - Nehemiah had the opportunity to think **first** about saving his skin when he heard about the plot against him in Nehemiah 6:10. He had no way of knowing he was being set up. But he refused to put himself first (v. 11)...and passed!

The Test: Will Nehemiah put God or himself first?

Answer: God

Score: 100%

The Result: He didn't die and God's Temple got completed.

8. Esther - Esther had a chance to be selfish and not put it all on the line for the Jews in Esther 4:14. But in verse 16 she put her own self interests aside and took a stand for God's people.

The Test: Will Esther put God or herself first?

Answer: God

Score: 100%

The Result: No one dies although there was clearly the potential for it.

9. Jesus - In the garden Jesus requested that He be released from having to die for Man's sins. His Father denied the request. He had "learned obedience" and **we** benefitted from it!

The Test: Will Jesus put His Father's will or His first?

Answer: His Father's

Score:
1,000,000,000,000,000,000,000,000,000,000,000%!

The Result: We don't have to die in our sins.

There seem to be a few constants to these tests. The main factor in failure seems to be **pride**. That is not surprising. Job 41:34 tells us that the devil (Leviathan) is the **king** over the children of pride. You can be saved and still have the devil for your king if you are given to pride. You will go to Heaven when you die but your life's decisions will be those that the devil desires you to make.

God doesn't seem to take failure too personal. No one went to Hell for failing. With Adam he simply acknowledged the failure and then promptly made them animal skins for clothing. With David He stated that David had only ever turned aside from God in the matter of Uriah. Why was his numbering of Israel not considered turning from what God had commanded Him? Because, in a test, God simply distances Himself from the testee and gives **no** advice or direction. He had given David no directive. He was watching to see what David would do on his own. That's why it's a test!

None of these people seemed to ever suspect they were being tested. Nor did they realize all that was on the line.

Questions you Should be Asking

There are several questions that should come to your mind concerning **your test**.

1. Will God tell me when it's coming?

No. If He told you when it was coming then you would prepare yourself and that very preparation would negate the results of the test.

2. Will God help me through it?

No. Again, if God helped you then it wouldn't be **you** who passed the test.

3. Is there anything I can look for to recognize that it's coming?

No. The circumstances are different in each case. Although Jacob and Nehemiah were aware of imminent danger, the others were not. Adam was living in Edenic splendor. David was a great and successful king. Esther was a Queen at the height of her power. No, there can be no warning signs to allow you to prepare. You can **never know** when the test is coming. Therefore, you realize how important it is that you be always in **top spiritual shape** so as to be able to make the right decision without knowing that you are being tested.

4. Will I know when it's over?

No. God told **us** in the Bible but He never told the testees that they had just passed or failed His ultimate test. So, if you have been reading this and saying, "Oh yeah! I remember. That time back there must have been mine." This just shows how truly shallow you are. You need help! Keep reading.

But this doesn't mean you can't prepare. Think of yourself as a lone soldier walking cautiously through an enemy village. There is **one** enemy soldier who is going to attack you but you cannot know when or where. You only know that the struggle will be hand-to-hand. What can you do? Obviously you will want to keep yourself in top physical shape. (1 Cor. 9:27) You will also want to make sure you are not carrying any unnecessary weight that would slow your reactions. (Heb. 12:1) You will also always be alert to that one, single, constant danger.
(1 Peter 1:10, 11) Above all, you will not want to lose this coming encounter.

Fortunately, there are a few things you **can do** to prepare yourself for this coming test. These are things that will **work against your pride** and help to **keep you in good spiritual shape**.

1. Stay in church - Being in church is good for you. Now I'm talking about a good, fundamental, King James Bible believing church. Being preached to will help you keep your flesh, your pride, in check. The sound of God's words entering your ears as they are being preached will have a good effect on your heart. Also, if you get to one of those times in the Christian life when you're mad at your pastor, and you humble yourself, shut up, and stay in church, **that** in itself will be good for beating down your devilish pride. **Stay in church!**

2. Submerge yourself in your Bible - Again, as you read God's holy words **on a daily basis** they will have a good effect on your heart. They will suppress your natural wickedness and strengthen you spiritually. There is no way to explain how valuable daily Bible reading is to the Christian.

3. Don't feed your ego - Don't allow yourself to get caught up in the "greatness" of your accomplishments. Whether they are job, sports or ministry related, do the best you can but then go on without looking back to savor your "greatness". My great college professor once told us, “Don’t read your own reviews.” In other words, don’t believe everything good people say about you. It will go to your head...or heart.

4. Accept humiliation - We all **love** to talk about being “humble”. But the fact is that we **hate** being humiliated. But face the facts, we all do or say some dumb things and are therefore embarrassed by them. Accept it. It is good for your pride.

5. Be prepared - How? Two ways. First get rid of the things in your life that feed your flesh. You may excuse questionable music, jokes, clothing, entertainment or habits but they only strengthen your flesh and weaken your spiritual resolve. Also, rid your life of your “secret sins.” You know exactly what I’m talking about. Second, you may want to listen to preaching tapes, or solemn music or dress in a conservative wardrobe. You don’t have to be Amish. You don’t have to drive a horse and buggy or move to a compound on top of a mountain. But you would do well to be a step or two out of sync with the world. The world’s heart should not be your heart. You can enjoy the blessing of living in America without selling yourself out to it.

His Ultimate Pleasure

If your common, daily sacrifices are a pleasure to God, think what a blessing it would be to Him for you to make the right choice in your test. If our daily sacrifices represent a constant horizon on a graph, then passing “The Test” would be a “spike”, a mountain peak of pleasure in your life. What Christian wouldn’t desire that? Do you desire it enough to prepare yourself?

CHAPTER NINE

When It's All Over

Where will you be 10,000 years from now? 100,000? 10 million? You **will** be someplace. If you haven't accepted Jesus Christ as your Saviour then you will be burning eternally in the Lake of Fire. If you are saved you will be eternally enjoying fellowship with God. And what will your own, personal, special benefits be in eternity? They will be those rewards you earned while on this planet during this remarkably brief period in your existence called, "life."

A little Mind Exercise

As you know, eternity has no beginning and no end. If eternity was represented by a line moving left-to-right it would be endless. Look to your left and you can see no place that is its starting point. Look to your right and you can see no point of termination. Now try this. Look to your left and imagine eternity **past** stretching out endless. You see past the time of Christ, back beyond Abraham's life, back past Noah and then

Adam an then you enter the eternity before time and yet it goes on. There is no earth, stars or solar systems. Just God. Now look to your right and imagine eternity **future**. The Blessed Hope, when we are taken live up into Heaven, the Tribulation which we will fortunately miss, the millennial reign of Christ, and then the New Heaven and the New Earth and then stretching out beyond you 10,000 years, 100,000 years, 100 million

It represents the brief "instant" in eternity that you have to garner some rewards for serving your Creator.

years and then **more!** What will your rewards be out there? Whatever it is it will be whatever rewards you can earn while on this earth in a life that the Bible limits to 70 years and James relates to being no more than a vapor. Now, bend this page so that you can see the edge of the paper. Do you know what you're looking at? With **eternity past** stretching endlessly to the left of the page and **eternity future** stretching endlessly to its right, the thin edge of the page of this book represents **your 70 year life span on earth** in all of your eternal existence. It represents the brief "instant" in eternity that you have to garner some rewards for serving your Creator. You say, "But I don't serve Him for rewards." Right, No one should. We should serve Him because we love, appreciate and worship Him. **But**, if we are successful at that, the rewards come along anyway. Now, look again at the edge of the page. What personal pleasure could be so great that you would sacrifice the eternal pleasure you could have by living in such a way that you pleased your Creator daily. Look at the page! If you could spend your entire 70 years in ecstacy it would still amount to a blink of an eye in eternity. Will you sacrifice 500 million years of ecstacy for a few years here of living for yourself?

Impressing God

God will not be impressed with your golf trophy. He will not care about your "ten-point buck". Your titles in life, your monetary worth, your lauding by other humans. He will only look back at everyday of your life to see what you did to please Him. What did you do? If you just said, "I won souls." then I suggest you throw this book away and go "soul winning, soul winning, soul winning" for you are incapable of comprehending the greatest achievement you could attain. Just go soul winning and hope for the best.

If you want to be a pleasure to God what should you do? First, don't use this book as an excuse to **not** win souls. I am not saying we shouldn't win souls. I am simply trying to point out that winning souls is **not** the premiere thing a Christian can do. Or was meant to do. Today we have soul winners who are liars, thieves and bed-hoppers. How do they justify such wickedness? By claiming that the most important thing we can do is win souls. They win souls so any **wrong** they do simply doesn't compare to the "great good" they are doing in their mind. **But**, if we are here to live our daily lives in a holy, chaste manner so as to be a daily pleasure to our Creator then **more than soul winning** will be required of us. Of course, these immoral soul winners realize this, so they will be fierce in their attempt to sway anyone from getting "carried away" with holy living. It may even be seen as a hindrance to soul winning.

Beyond Soul Winning

Soul winning is good, but there is more, much more. There are by all means higher levels and greater goals to be reached than one human rescuing another from God. But these require sacrifice on our part. It may cause us discomfort. It may bring down the wrath of soul winners with closets full of bones to hide. But you'd better believe that God didn't put man on this earth just so He could damn him and then send out an army of soul winners to see how many they can redeem. God put man here to put a smile on His face. He put him in a perfect environment and then tested him to see if he **really** loved Him more than himself. It's been downhill from there! But this great God was willing to show His own love for His creation by coming down here and dying for him. Surely **that** should motivate His creatures to want to please Him. Then He gave him a Book so that he would know exactly how to please Him. (Of course, if man doesn't **read** that Book he can never know how to please his Creator.) Now He waits. He sees one get saved and He watches to see if he'll grow. Will he rid his life of "that"? Will he get into church? Will he say "No" to himself and stop doing "that"? Will he read the Book that He gave him? Will he pass his test?

Don't stop soul winning. But don't stop **at** soul winning. Realize that there is far more expected and required of you if you are going to be a successful child of God. You are going to have to put a smile on His face, daily. And soul winning will **not** cover for all that you lack in your life. And if you lose your way, if you lose your direction, if you wonder just for a moment what you're here for, you need only consult one single verse of that great Book to get your bearings and set you straight on your way through life.

Thou art worthy, O Lord, to receive glory and honour and power:
for thou hast created all things, and *for thy pleasure* they are and were created.

Index One
Scripture References

Old Testament

Index Two
General

-D-

-E-

-F-

-I-

-J-

-K-

-L-

-M-

-N-

-O-

-P-

-Q-

-R-

-S-

Gipp's Understandable History of the Bible

A textbook size book that covers the history of the Bible from its conception, through history and into our hands. Written in a simple to understand manner and easily read format. This is a great book for either a new convert or a seasoned Christian who wishes to gain further knowledge of how we got our Bible.

ISBN: 1-890120-27-8 $24.99

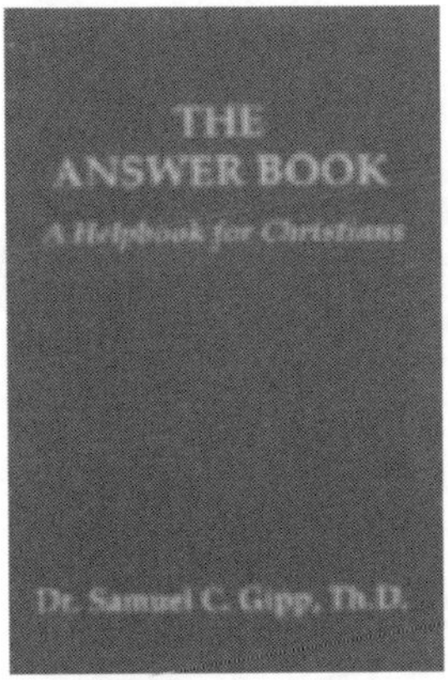

The Answer Book

The 62 questions most asked by King James Bible critics, and their answers. Laid out so the average Christian can answer the attacks. Great for the college student whose faith is being attacked by his school's faculty.

ISBN: 1-890120-00-6 $6.99

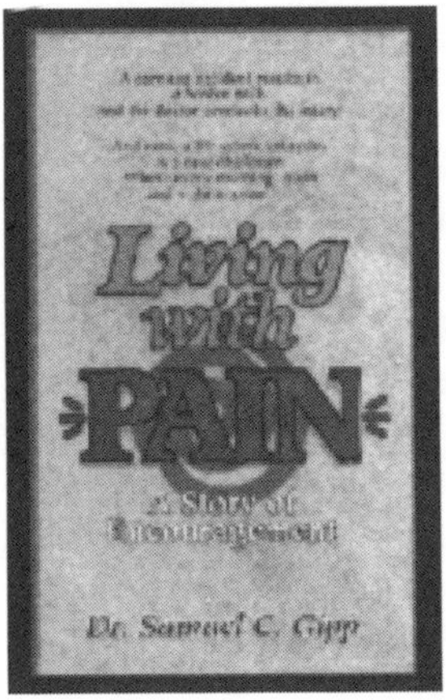

Living With Pain

Samuel C. Gipp, 23 years of age, had recently graduated from Bible college and had entered the field of evangelism. Through an unfortunate accident, which left him with a broken neck, this was postponed for a year. Misdiagnosed he went almost three months before it was surgically corrected. But his ordeal was just beginning. Since that day he has lived a life filled with constant pain. This book has been a great comfort to those who suffer from chronic pain.

ISBN: 1-890120-02-2 $3.99

Check out our Webpage at: www.samgipp.com

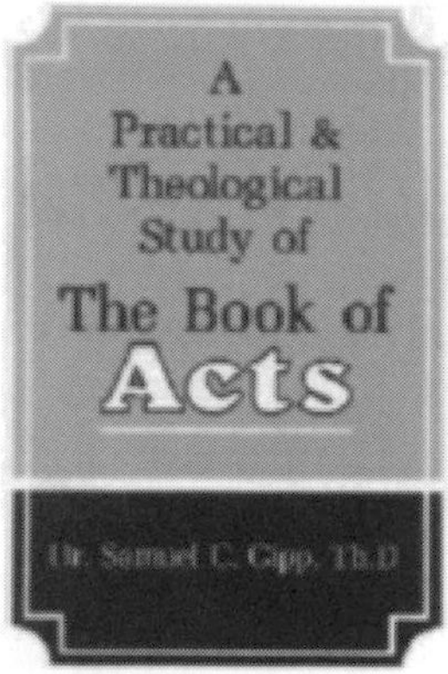

A Practical and Theological Study of the Book of Acts

Dr. Gipp takes a difficult and sometimes misunderstood book of the Bible and lays it out in an easy to understand manner. The confusion of tongues is dealt with as is the so-called "error" of the translation of "Easter" in Acts 12. A great study help for Bible studies or Sunday School classes.

ISBN: 1-890120-06-5 $19.99

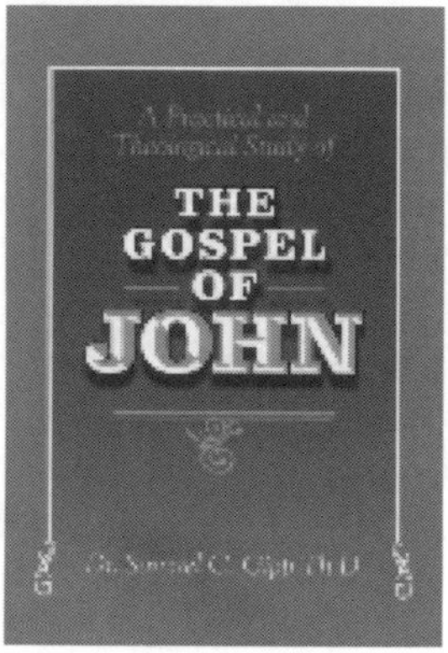

A Practical and Theological Study of the Gospel of John

This study explores the martial skills of the Lord Jesus Christ as He engages and defeats His adversaries time after time. Further subjects are the "wine" of chapter 2 and the authentication for the beginning of chapter 8. A book that will help the teacher as well as the student of Scripture.

ISBN: 1-890120-11-1 $19.99

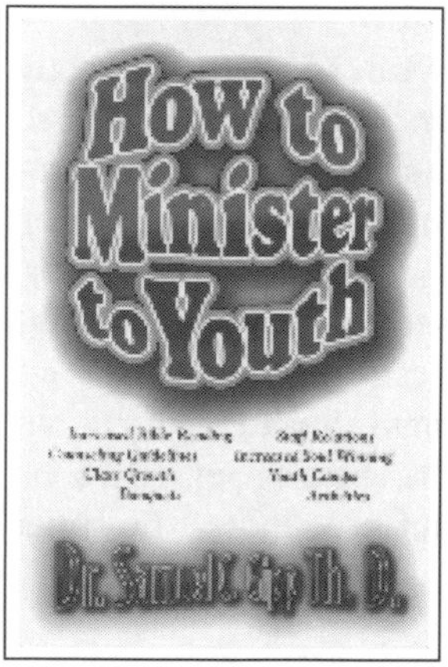

How To Minister To Youth

Dr. Gipp took a problem ridden youth department and built it into a Bible reading, soul winning, dedicated group of young people.

In addition to ideas and instructions on youth camps, banquets, soul winning, and a list of skits and activities, this book tells how to deal with "hard cases" and troubled youth groups. A must for every pastor and youth group leader.

ISBN: 1-890120-07-3 $14.99

To order these books or receive a free catalog contact:
DayStar Publishing • P. O. Box 464 • Miamitown, OH 45041

Life After Y2K

In this book Dr. Gipp discusses the shameful seven year panic that preceded January 1, 2000. While rebuking Christians for their lack of faith, Dr. Gipp comes down more harshly on the real instigator of the panic, the News Industry.

More importantly, Dr. Gipp tells the reader how to keep from being caught up in the next coming "crisis" which is being planned even now.

ISBN:1-890120-10-3 $3.99

Reading and Understanding the Variations Between the Critical Apparatuses of Nestle's 25th and 26th Editions of the Novum Testamentum-Graece

A technical work to be used with the Nestle-Aland Greek New Testament, suitable for individual or classroom study. This second edition also addresses the changes in the 27th edition of Nestle.

ISBN: 1-890120-16-2 $14.99

Selected Sermons, Vol. 1-10

Each volume in this series highlights five of Dr. Gipp's most requested sermons. Over 30 years of preaching have gone into these works. These messages are still being used of God to His glory.

ISBN:

Volume 1 1-890120-08-1 $14.99 each

Volume 2 1-890120-14-6

Volume 3 1-890120-17-0

Call in your order at: **1-800-311-1823**